HANDBOOK

OF THE

ITALIAN ARMY.

PREPARED BY THE GENERAL STAFF.

1913.

The Naval & Military Press Ltd

Published by

The Naval & Military Press Ltd
Unit 10 Ridgewood Industrial Park,
Uckfield, East Sussex,
TN22 5QE England

Tel: +44 (0) 1825 749494
Fax: +44 (0) 1825 765701

www.naval-military-press.com
www.military-genealogy.com

In reprinting in facsimile from the original, any imperfections are inevitably reproduced and the quality may fall short of modern type and cartographic standards.

CONTENTS.

INTRODUCTION.

	PAGE
Area and population	13
Government	13
Religion and education	14
Development of the military forces	14-16

CHAPTER I.
COMPOSITION OF THE FORCES. CONDITIONS OF SERVICE. NUMBERS AVAILABLE IN PEACE AND WAR.

Composition of the forces	17
Conditions of service	17
Terms of service in various categories	18
Strength of various categories	18
Re-engagement	19
Imigrants	20
Rejections	20
Distribution of recruits	21
Peculiarities of the system	21
Peace and war strengths	22
Miscellaneous organizations	23

CHAPTER II.
ADMINISTRATION.

Central	24
The Minister for War	24
The War Office	24-25
Councils and committees	26
Local administration	27

CHAPTER III.
STAFF.

The general staff	28
The staff corps	28

PAGE

CHAPTER III—STAFF—*continued.*

Functions of chief of the general staff 28
Organization and distribution at headquarters ... 29–30
Personnel 31
Uniform :—
  General officers 31
  Officers of the staff corps 32–33

CHAPTER IV.

ORGANIZATION AND MOBILIZATION.

Peace :—
  Composition of active army 34
  Army commander 35
  Army corps commander 35
  Cavalry divisional commander 35
  Infantry ,, ,, ... 35
  Infantry and cavalry brigade commanders 35
  Field artillery commands 36
  Fortress artillery commanders 36
  Artillery directions 36
  Engineer commands 37
  ,, directions 37
  Commissariat directions 37
  Medical directions 37
  Inspectors general ... ...
    (*a*) Cavalry 37
    (*b*) Artillery 38
    (*c*) Mountain troops 38
    (*d*) Engineers 38
    (*e*) Medical services 39
    (*f*) Commissariat services 39
    (*g*) Directorate of experiments 39
  Military districts 39
    Organization 39
    Personnel 40
    Duties 40
  Mobile militia 40
  Territorial militia 41
War :—
  Subdivision of forces 41
  Staff of an army 42
  Army corps 42

CHAPTER IV—ORGANIZATION AND MOBILIZATION—*continued.*

	PAGE
Cavalry division	43
Infantry „	43
Mountain troops	43–44
Mobilization :—	
Preparation of mobilization scheme	44
System of mobilization	45
Rate of mobilization	45–46

CHAPTER V.
OFFICERS AND NON-COMMISSIONED OFFICERS.

Officers of the active army (categories)	47
Recruitment of officers	47
Age of retirement of officers	47
Reserve of officers	47
Non-commissioned officers	49

CHAPTER VI.
CARABINIERI REALI.

Peace :—
Organization	50
Staff	50
Territorial legions	50
King's bodyguard	50
Establishment of territorial legions	51
Recruit legion	52
Establishment of recruit legion	52–53

War :—
Organization	53

Uniform :—
King's bodyguard	54
Carabinieri	54
Armament and equipment	54
Ammunition	54
Non-commissioned officers	55
General remarks	55

CHAPTER VII.
INFANTRY.

Organization :—
Infantry of the line	56
Peace establishment	57–59
War „	60

CHAPTER VII—INFANTRY—*continued.*

<table>
<tr><td></td><td>PAGE</td></tr>
<tr><td>Bersaglieri :—</td><td></td></tr>
<tr><td> Peace establishment</td><td>60</td></tr>
<tr><td> Distribution</td><td>61</td></tr>
<tr><td>Alpine Infantry (" Alpini ") :—</td><td></td></tr>
<tr><td> Recruitment</td><td>61</td></tr>
<tr><td> Peace establishment</td><td>62</td></tr>
<tr><td>Uniform :—</td><td></td></tr>
<tr><td> Grenadiers and infantry of the line</td><td>63–64</td></tr>
<tr><td> Bersaglieri</td><td>64</td></tr>
<tr><td> " Alpini "</td><td>65</td></tr>
<tr><td>Badges of rank</td><td>65–66</td></tr>
<tr><td>Armament and Equipment :—</td><td></td></tr>
<tr><td> Infantry of the Line</td><td>66–68</td></tr>
<tr><td> Grenadiers</td><td>66–68</td></tr>
<tr><td> Bersaglieri</td><td>66–68</td></tr>
<tr><td> " Alpini "</td><td>66–68</td></tr>
<tr><td> Bersaglieri cyclists</td><td>68</td></tr>
<tr><td>Rations. *See* Appendix V.</td><td></td></tr>
<tr><td>Regimental Transport :—</td><td></td></tr>
<tr><td> Infantry of the Line and Bersaglieri</td><td>68</td></tr>
<tr><td> " Alpini "</td><td>69</td></tr>
<tr><td>Entrenching tools</td><td>70</td></tr>
<tr><td>Disciplinary companies and military penal establishments</td><td>71</td></tr>
</table>

CHAPTER VIII.
CAVALRY.

<table>
<tr><td>Organization</td><td>72</td></tr>
<tr><td>Peace establishments</td><td>73–74</td></tr>
<tr><td>War establishment</td><td>74</td></tr>
<tr><td>Specially trained N.C.Os. and men</td><td>75</td></tr>
<tr><td>Uniform</td><td>75</td></tr>
<tr><td>Armament</td><td>77</td></tr>
<tr><td>Equipment</td><td>78</td></tr>
<tr><td>Regimental transport</td><td>78</td></tr>
<tr><td>Rations. *See* Appendix V.</td><td></td></tr>
<tr><td>Tools and explosives</td><td>78</td></tr>
</table>

CHAPTER IX.
ARTILLERY.

<table>
<tr><td>Composition</td><td>79</td></tr>
<tr><td>Horse Artillery :—</td><td></td></tr>
<tr><td> Organization</td><td>79</td></tr>
<tr><td> Peace and war establishments</td><td>80</td></tr>
</table>

PAGE

CHAPTER IX—ARTILLERY—*continued.*

Field Artillery :—
    Organization 80-81
    Peace and war establishments 82
Mountain Artillery :—
    Organization 82
    Peace and war establishments... 83
Heavy Field Artillery :—
    Organization 84
    Peace and War establishments 84
Fortress Artillery :—
    Organization 84
    Peace and war establishments... 84
Technical service of artillery 86
Uniform 87
Armament :—
    Details of field and mountain guns 87-89
    „   „   howitzers 88-89
    „   fortress artillery 85
    Personnel 89
Equipment... 90
Ammunition per gun (war) 90
Small arm ammunition 91
Regimental Transport :—
    Field artillery battery 91
    Mountain battery 91
Entrenching tools... 91
General remarks 91

CHAPTER X.

PART I.—ENGINEERS.

Organization 92
Peace establishments 93-94
War organization and strength 95-96
Units furnished by mobile militia 97
Territorial militia 97
Uniform 97
Armament and equipment 98
Bridging material :—
    Divisional pontoon section 98
    Bridging train 99
Transport 99-100
Entrenching tools... 100

CHAPTER X—*continued.*

PART II.—AVIATION.

	PAGE
General description	101-102
Organization of aeroplanes and dirigibles	102
Types of aeroplanes and dirigibles	102-103
Docks for dirigibles	103
Telephotography	104
Aviation courses	104
Uniform	104
Extra duty pay	104-105
Portable hangars	105-106
Headquarters of aeroplane squadrons	106
Aeroplane parks	106

CHAPTER XI.
MACHINE GUNS.

Organization	107
Peace establishments	107
War ,,	107-108
Ammunition	108
Armament	108

CHAPTER XII.
THE INTENDANCE, COMMISSARIAT AND ADMINISTRATION CORPS.

The Intendance Corps:—	
Peace organization and duties	109
War organization	109-110
The Commissariat Corps:—	
Organization and peace establishment	110-111
Commissariat officers	111
Supply companies	112
War organization and strength	112-114
The Corps of Administration:—	
Duties	114
Composition	114
Uniform	115
Armament	115

CHAPTER XIII.
THE MEDICAL AND VETERINARY CORPS.

The Medical Corps:—	
Peace establishment	116
Medical officers, regular	116
,, ,, complementary	116
Peace organization	117

	PAGE
CHAPTER XIII—THE MEDICAL AND VETERINARY CORPS—*contd.*	
War organization	117
Peace and war establishments	117–118
Uniform	119
Armament	119
The Italian Red Cross Society:—	
Personnel	119
War organization	120
Work in peace	120
The Veterinary Corps:—	
Officers	120
Organization	121

CHAPTER XIV.
THE TRANSPORT.

Composition	122
Peace establishment of a company	122
War organization	122–123
Efficiency of the system in war	123
Uniform, equipment, armament	123–124
Motor cars	123–124
Mechanical transport	123–124

CHAPTER XV.
HORSE SUPPLY.

Census returns	125
Peace requirements	125
War „	125
Quality of horses	125
Breeding establishments and remount depôts	125–126
Purchase of horses	126
Officers' chargers	127
Mobilization arrangements	127
Expenditure	127
Mules	127

CHAPTER XVI.
EDUCATIONAL ESTABLISHMENTS.

Military colleges	128
The military school	128
The military academy	129
School of musketry	130
Cavalry school	130
School for sub-lieutenants of artillery and engineers	131
Army medical school	131
School of gunnery	132
The staff college	132
Courses of instruction	133–134

CHAPTER XVII.

FINANCE AND PAY.

The Budget:—
Ordinary expenditure	135
Extraordinary expenditure	136
Officers, pay of	136
Officers' allowances	137–138
,, pensions	138

N.C.Os. and Rank and File:—
Pay of	139
Carabinieri pay of	139
Extra duty pay	139
Pensions	140

CHAPTER XVIII.

INSTRUCTION AND TRAINING.

Annual course of training	141
Details of the course	141
Infantry	141–143
Cavalry	144
Artillery	145
War games and lectures	146
Staff tours	146
Local training and manœuvres	146
Army manœuvres	146–147

CHAPTER XIX.

TACTICS.

Infantry Formations:—
The section	148
The company	148
The battalion, regiment and brigade	149
Machine guns	149

Cavalry Formations:—
The troop	149
The squadron	150
The regiment	150
The brigade	151
The division	152
Action, dismounted	152

Artillery Formations:—
The battery	152
The brigade	153

Chapter XIX—Tactics—continued.

	PAGE
Infantry tactics	153-154
Cavalry „	155-156
Artillery „	156-157
General tactical tendencies of the army	157-158

CHAPTER XX.
Reconnaissance, Protection, Marches, and Camping Arrangements.

General Remarks	159
Reconnaissance and protection	159
Distant reconnaissance	159
Near reconnaissance	159
Cavalry reconnaissance	160
Reconnaissance by other arms	160
Protection on the march	161
Outposts	162-165
March outposts	165
Marches	165
Rate of marching	165
Halts	166
Length of marches	166
Automobiles	167
Transport	167
March orders	168
Billets	168
Camps	169
Bivouacs	169
Table of lengths of column of troops on the march, and camping spaces required	170

CHAPTER XXI.
Permanent Defences and Communications.

Land defences—organization of	171
Table showing distribution	171-172
Maritime defences—organization and distribution	173
Communications	173
Telephones and telegraphs	173
Railways	174-175
Roads	175
Canals	175

CHAPTER XXII.

COLONIAL TROOPS.

	PAGE
Libya :—	
Provisional arrangements	176
Erithrea :—	
General description of troops	177
Composition of units	177–178
Approximate total strength	178
Recruiting	178
Pay	179
Characteristics of native troops	180
Arms, equipment, and uniform	180
Administration	180
Italian Somaliland :—	
General description of troops...	180
Officers	181
Rank and file	181

APPENDICES.

I.	Composition and distinguishing colours of infantry brigades	182
II.	Peace stations of Alpine troops	184
III.	Organization into commands and districts	186
IV.	Small-arm ammunition	188
V.	Rations and forage	189
VI.	Peace stations of cavalry	192
VII.	Organization of the fortress artillery	194
VIII.	Engineers, peace stations...	195
IX.	Working of administrative services	196
X.	Vocabulary...	198
XI.	Weights and measures	204

IN POCKET AT END OF BOOK.

SKETCH MAP OF ITALY SHOWING DISTRIBUTION OF ARMY.

HANDBOOK

OF THE

ITALIAN ARMY.

INTRODUCTION.

Area and Population.

The kingdom of Italy has an area of 110,659 square miles* of which 91,418 belong to the mainland and 19,241 to Sardinia and Sicily. The extent of the French frontier is 304, of the Swiss 420 and of the Austro-Hungarian 487 miles, or a total land frontier of 1,211 miles.

The resident population (1st January, 1908) amounted to 33,910,000 or about 306 inhabitants to the square mile. The number of foreigners was 61,600 of whom 11,616 were Austrians, 10,757 Swiss, 10,745 Germans, 8,768 English, 6,953 French. The population is now estimated at over 35,000,000.

A large and increasing number of Italians emigrate every year, principally to America. There is also an Italian colony of over 100,000 in Tunis. At least half of these emigrants return to Italy when they have made sufficient money. In 1900 the number of emigrants was 352,782, in 1907 the figures had risen to 700,469.

Government.

The form of government is a constitutional monarchy, legislative power being exercised collectively by the King, the Senate and the Chamber of Deputies. The executive

---

* According to the figures of the Italian Survey Department.

power belongs solely to the King, who is the supreme head of the State, commands all the military and naval forces, makes treaties and declares war. Any treaty affecting the finances or territory of the State must be ratified by the two Chambers.

The *Senate* is composed of the Royal Princes (if over 21 years of age) and of an unlimited number of life members of over 40 years of age, nominated by the King from among persons who have attained positions of distinction. In 1910 the Senate numbered 364, exclusive of Royal Princes.

The *Chamber* is composed of 508 members who must be over 30 years of age and who are chosen by the electoral divisions.

Religion and Education.

The Roman Catholic Church is, nominally, the ruling State religion of Italy, but the power of the Church is subordinated to the civil government, and there is freedom of worship for the adherents of all recognized creeds. 97 per cent. of the population profess the Roman Catholic religion while 65,000 people or ·2 per cent. of the population belong to various evangelical Protestant denominations.

The State regulates public instruction and maintains, in conjunction with the provincial administration, public schools of every grade. Only the lower grade of elementary education is compulsory. The educational authorities have had great difficulties to contend with owing to the high percentage of illiterates and the dearth of good teachers. Considerable progress has, however, been made during the last 40 years: the percentage of illiterates, which was 73·5 in 1862 had fallen to 52·1 in 1901, and there has been an increase of 121 per cent. in school attendance.

Development of the Military Forces.

The Sardinian Army.—After the unification of Italy in 1861, King Victor Emmanuel and his advisers based the organization of the new Italian Army (and constitution) on the Sardinian models.

The Sardinian Army was composed of a nucleus of volunteers, supplemented by a contingent of conscripts chosen by lot. The Army was divided into a first line, in which the term of service varied from five to eight years, and a second line, in which men were liable to service for 11 years: the training of the second line was limited to four periods of 6 months each. With an army organized on these lines King Charles Albert put 60,000 men into the field in 1848 and, prior to his defeat at Novara in the following year, had increased that number to 95,000. In 1859, when hostilities again broke out with Austria, the Sardinian Field Army at first amounted to 60,000 men, with 25,000 in reserve formations. Before the end of the war the numbers were increased to 110,000. This was the last appearance of a Sardinian Army and, thanks to the talent for organization shown by General de la Marmora, it was more efficient than any of its predecessors.

Organization of 1860-4.—After the unification of Italy the elements which had to be welded together into one army consisted of the following :—

(a) The Sardinian army 110,000 strong.
(b) Officers and soldiers of Italian origin, released from the Austrian service: number 37,500.
(c) Army of the league : this was chiefly composed of volunteers with no settled organization : number 31,500.
(d) The Tuscan army : about 20,000 men.
(e) The Neapolitan army, which was still showing the effects of its defeat by Garibaldi : strength about 60,000.
(f) The Chasseurs of the Tiber : 1,600 strong.
(g) The army of the south, many of whom were irregulars or deserters from regular corps : strength 44,000.

In addition to these soldiers already serving, conscription was applied to the whole of Italy. Every Italian citizen on attaining the age of 20 was liable to serve either in the first category, in which the term of service was for five years with the colours and for six in the reserve, or in the second category, the men in which remained on unlimited leave but were liable to be called up for five years. The employment of paid substitutes was allowed.

Under this system an army with a war strength of 360,000 men was organized of which 273,000 were infantry and 19,000 cavalry. There was little uniformity, however, as the various local armies were to a great extent autonomous, and there existed no organization higher than an infantry or cavalry brigade.

Organization of 1870–6.—These six years mark a period of transition in which General Ricotti broke away from the traditions of the old Sardinian army and laid the foundations of an Italian army on a national basis. The following were the more important reforms introduced by this Minister :—

(*a*) The grouping of the army into 10 Army Corps.
(*b*) The division of the country into seven territorial *circonscriptions*.
(*c*) The adoption of a system of national, instead of regional, recruiting.
(*d*) The obligation of all Italian citizens to serve in one or another of the military formations from their twentieth to their thirty-ninth year.
(*e*) The creation of a mobile militia and of a territorial militia.
(*f*) The admission, on payment of a cash fee, of one-year volunteers.

Since 1876 various laws for the reform of the army have been passed of which the general tendency has been gradually to decrease the period of colour service and to lessen the number of heads under which service could be evaded. The number of Army Corps has been increased from 10 to 12, but in spite of these and other reforms the condition of the army remained unsatisfactory—mainly owing to the parsimony of the Treasury. To remedy this a Commission of Inquiry sat from 1908–10 and as a result of its recommendations various reforms were introduced by General Spingardi (in 1910) which form the basis of the present system.

CHAPTER I.

COMPOSITION OF THE FORCES. CONDITIONS OF SERVICE. NUMBERS AVAILABLE IN PEACE AND WAR.

Composition of the Forces.

The military forces of Italy are grouped into:—
(*a*) The active army.
(*b*) The mobile militia (milizia mobile).
(*c*) The territorial militia (milizia territoriale).
(*d*) Volunteer corps.
(*e*) Customs guards.
(*f*) Colonial troops (*see* Chap. XXII).

Conditions of Service.

Every Italian citizen capable of bearing arms is liable to military service from the end of his twentieth to the end of his thirty-ninth year. In case of emergency the former limit may be anticipated. Men fit for service born in any one year are called the 'class' of that year : thus the men liable for service in 1912 are called the 1892 class.

Levy councils assemble annually in the chief towns of military districts, under the supervision of the recruiting commission, and verify the lists of young men in their twentieth year, which are submitted by the local civil authorities. The men having balloted for numbers, the councils decide which are fit for service, which shall be put back to the next levy as temporarily unfit or below the standard, and which shall be discharged outright as medically unfit. Substitutes are not allowed.

This having been completed, the recruits fit for service are divided into three categories. The terms of service in each category are shown in the following table :—

Categories.	Active Army.		Mobile Militia.	Terrtl. Militia.	Total.
	With the Colours.	On permanent furlough.			
1st Category ...	2	6	4	7	19
2nd Category ...	—	8	4	7	19
3rd Category ...	—	—	—	19	19

The strength of the various categories varies every year. The total of the 1st category of the 1889 class after rejections, exemptions and relegations was 151,839.

Of these, 5,021 were already under arms as officers, cadets, &c., 11,996 were absent without leave, and 16,490 were exempted for various reasons, such as residence abroad, incorporated in the Customs Guards, &c., leaving 118,469 to be assigned to corps.

The 2nd category was 34,079, and the 3rd category, 26,977.

Until the year 1910, the period of service with the colours was nominally 3 years. As a matter of fact, infantrymen rarely served for more than 2 years ; the cavalry and artillery, however, served for 3 years and there was considerable opposition in military circles to reducing the colour service for those arms.

In 1910, the War Minister, General Spingardi introduced a Bill to establish a 2 years' period of service for all arms. This was passed by Parliament, it being considered that the mounted branches would not suffer materially in efficiency if a nucleus of re-enlisted men was retained with the colours and if recruits were selected from men who already knew something about horses and equitation.

The 1st category is composed of men, physically fit, who have no legal claim for exemption from military service. Its strength is fixed annually by Act of Parliament.

Should the number of men in the 1st category be in excess of the strength fixed by Parliament, the War Minister has the power of granting extraordinary leave, in anticipation of the period of permanent furlough, to a proportionate number of recruits who are designated by the numbers drawn in the levy ballot. Preference is given to men put back for 2 years and then those put back for 1 year. These recruits must, however, do 3 months' training during the first year and must come out for training as reservists during the second year. The number of men in excess is now between 10,000 and 15,000 per annum, but it is hoped in the near future to increase the peace strength sufficiently to enable these men to be absorbed.

When men of the 1st category are sent on unlimited leave, their names and mobilization centres are sent to the civil authorities of their district.

The *2nd category* is recruited from men in excess of those required for the 1st category, who drew the highest numbers in the ballot. Men belonging to this category may be, and usually are, called to the colours for training one or more times up to a total period of 12 months.

The *3rd category* is formed of those recruits who are exempt for family reasons from military service.

Men on permanent furlough and militiamen of all classes are liable to be called up for periodical terms of training. The number called up depends on financial consideration: the tendency of late years has been to increase it. In 1909 the figures were as follows :—

Active Army.	Mobile Militia.	Territorial Militia.	Total.
61,000	20,000	5,000	86,000

The period of training was from 20 to 30 days.

Volunteers.—Recruits of over 17 years of age, if of good character, and who have fired the eight regulation courses of musketry, are permitted to volunteer for 3 years' service, or for service in the 1st instead of in the 3rd category.

The tax on one-year volunteers is £80 for cavalry and £60 for the other arms. Service as a one year volunteer does not establish any claims to promotion.

The number of volunteers is from 1,500 to 2,000 per annum.

In time of war, Italian citizens, if fit for service, may volunteer for the duration of the campaign.

All non-commissioned officers and men of good character may re-engage for successive periods of one year. Should these men belong to the cavalry or horse artillery they have certain privileges, firstly, they receive a bonus fixed annually by Parliament and, secondly, should they have a brother coming up for service, he has the right to claim to be placed in the second category.

The number of men re-engaging annually for one year is from 3,000 to 3,500.

Emigrants.—Men wishing to leave Italy must obtain the permission of the military authorities, if they are in their ninteenth year, or if they are on permanent furlough from either the active army or the mobile militia. All men leaving the country who are liable to service must communicate their address to the Italian consul in the country in which they reside.

Boys who were born abroad and reside there, missionaries and boys who, when under sixteen years of age, emigrated from Europe, are excused service in time of peace. This rule does not apply to Egypt, Tripoli, Tunis or any Italian colony.

In time of war all Italians liable to service must carry out their military obligations.

Rejections.—The number of rejections for physical unfitness is very large, amounting usually to about 20 per cent. of the number of youths who are of an age to serve.

Men are rejected if they are criminals, if they fail to satisfy the medical authorities as to their fitness for service, or if they do not reach the necessary standard of height and chest measurement (5 ft. $0\frac{3}{5}$ in. and $31\frac{1}{2}$ inches respectively). Men of 5 ft. $0\frac{1}{4}$ in. or under are rejected. Men between 5 ft. $0\frac{3}{5}$ in. and 5 ft. $0\frac{1}{4}$ in. will be put back one or two years for re-examination, and then rejected, unless they reach the height of 5 ft. $0\frac{3}{5}$ in.

The following are the figures for the 1st category of the 1889 class, called up in October, 1909, and released in September, 1911 :—

Description.	Number.	Percentage of whole.
Cancelled (criminals, men wrongly registered, &c.). ("Cancellati")	12,834	2·51
Medically unfit. ("Riformati")	108,794	21·29
Put back to next levy. ("Rimandati")	127,528	24·96
Failed to present themselves. ("Renitenti")	48,865	9·57
1st Category	151,839	29·72
2nd Category	34,079	6·67
3rd Category	26,977	5·28
Total...	510,916	—

Distribution of Recruits.

After making various deductions for men already enrolled as volunteers, emigrants, students, etc., and absentees, the 1889 class of recruits was distributed as follows :—

Grenadiers and infantry of the line	57,879
Bersaglieri	7,541
"Alpini"	6,454
Cavalry	14,308
Horse Artillery	491
Field Artillery and transport	13,549
Mountain ,,	1,677
Coast ,,	2,111
Fortress ,,	2,824
Engineers and transport	6,287
Carabinieri	1,285
Medical Corps	2,288
Subsistence Companies	1,775
	118,469

Peculiarities of the System.

Until Italy became one nation some 40 years ago, the country had been split up into a number of small kingdoms and principalities. A considerable amount of "regional" feeling resulted which, if it had been allowed to permeate the army, might have interfered with its military efficiency. To avoid this danger and to make the army into a single unity, a special system of recruiting was initiated, which is still in force.

Speaking generally, the cavalry, field and horse artillery and engineers draw their recruits from all parts of the country. Infantry and bersaglieri regiments recruit from certain districts, other than those in which they are quartered.

Such a system might give rise to considerable confusion on mobilization. To obviate this in the cavalry and infantry, which change garrisons periodically, reservists are allotted to garrisons and not to particular units. For some period before a regiment changes quarters it draws its recruits from the district to which it is going to move, so that in case of mobilization a large proportion of the reservists would come back to their old regiment. In the horse and field artillery it is arranged that mobilization should be regional as far as possible. In the "alpini," and the mountain and coast artillery, both the system of recruiting and the system of mobilization are regional.

For the greater part of the army the system is to recruit on the national system, that is to say to post recruits to units stationed in a different part of the country to that in which they live: mobilization, on the contrary, is on the regional system as far as can be arranged.

PEACE AND WAR STRENGTH. (TRAINED MEN.)

	Peace and War Strength.						
—	Infantry.	Cavalry.	Artillery.		Other arms and depts.	Other trained men available.	Total.
			Men.	Guns.			
(a) Peace	134,860	26,000	40,600	1,480	49,400	—	250,860
(e) War	(b) 566,000	(b) 18,000	(b) 39,000	(d) 2,320	(b) 77,000	(c) 400,000	1,100,000

(a) Budget strength, 1912.

(b) Approximate numbers of men of the active army and mobile militia incorporated in mobilized units at war establishment.

(c) Trained territorial militia. In addition about 1,500,000 totally untrained men are enrolled in the territorial militia.

(d) 2,086 field guns and 234 mountain guns.

(e) Active army and mobile militia. Figures difficult to verify owing to emigration and other causes.

Volunteer Corps.—The Volunteer Cyclist and Automobile Corps consists of about 2,000 trained members organized in companies and battalions from nearly all the large cities.

Cadet Corps.—There are about 20 battalions of cadet corps, all of varying strength.

Mounted Volunteers of Venetia.—There are detachments at Mestre, Padua, Vicenza, Udine, and Treviso.

Alpine Volunteers.—The battalion at Cadore has a strength of about 600.

Lagoon Volunteers.—These are at Venice.

"*Guardie di Finanza*" (Custom Guards).—There are some 23,000 of these, who in time of war would be organized into 23 battalions of from 3 to 6 companies each. These are fine men, hardy, active, and intelligent, and accustomed to hard work and exposure on the frontiers. They are probably little inferior to the "alpini."

CHAPTER II.

ADMINISTRATION.

Central.

The King is the supreme head of the military forces of the State. In time of war the King either himself assumes command of the army in the field, or entrusts the command to a general officer, who is styled the Supreme Commander. In time of peace the command of the army is temporarily delegated by the King to the Minister for War.

The Minister for War.—The Minister for War is appointed by the King on the recommendation of the Prime Minister, and he usually, though not invariably, goes out of office on a change of government; he is responsible to Parliament for all matters connected with the army. His parliamentary assistant is the Under-Secretary of State for War who is usually a general officer.

The War Office.—The War Office and its auxiliary branches are situated at Rome. The present organization dates from July, 1908. The following is a list of its various branches who are all under the Minister for War :—

Branch.	Divisions and Offices.	No. of Divisions.	No of Sections.
(a) Offices directly under the Secretary or Under-Secretary of State	(1) Civil Cabinet	1	1
	(2) Military Cabinet	1	3
	(3) Inspector of Veterinary Services	—	—
	(4) Editor of the "Rivista Militare"	—	—
(b) Directorate of general affairs	(1) General questions	—	—
	(2) War Office personnel, military law	1	2
	(3) Accounts	1	3
	(4) Musketry and physical training	—	1
	(5) Remounts	—	1

Branch.	Divisions and Offices.	No. of Divisions.	No. of Sections.
(c) Directorate of the personal services of combatant officers	(1) General questions (2) Division I : personnel (3) Division II : personnel (4) Mobilization lists	— 1 1 —	— 3 3 —
(d) Directorate of civilian personnel and pensions	(1) General questions (2) Civilian personnel (3) Pensions, interior economy, cash payments	— 1 1	— 3 3
(e) Directorate of artillery and engineer administration	(1) General questions (2) Artillery administration (3) Photo - lithographic laboratory (4) Engineer administration	— 1 — 1	— 4 — 4
(f) Directorate of logistic and administrative services	(1) General (2) Supply (3) Pay and allowances (4) Clothing, equipment and medical material (5) Barracks and transport (6) Administrative personnel	— 1 1 1 1 —	— 3 3 3 2 1
(g) Directorate of recruiting and troops	(1) General questions (2) Recruiting: Division I (3) Recruiting : Division II (4) Troops (5) Records and registers	— 1 1 1 1	— 4 4 4 2
(h) Directorate of audit of accounts	(1) General questions (2) Pay and allowances (3) Payment for materiel (4) Accounts of Army Corps and Divisions	— 1 1 1	— 2 3 2
	Total	21	64

Councils and Committees.

The Minister for War is further assisted by the following authorities :—

(1) *The Chief of the General Staff*, who is technical adviser to the War Minister on all points of military policy. (*See* p. 28).

(2) *The Supreme Committee of Defence.*—This Committee is charged with the study of all questions affecting the naval and military defence of the Kingdom and is especially intended to ensure unity of action between the Admiralty and War departments. It is presided over by the Prime Minister and consists of a number of effective and consultative members and of a secretariat. The effective members are the chief of the general staff, the general officers selected to command armies in case of war, the chief of the naval staff and the admiral selected to command the fleet on mobilization. The consultative members consist of various naval and military officers of high rank and the Secretaries of State for War and for the Navy.

(3.) *Army Council.*—This body is presided over by the War Minister and must meet at least three times in six months. Its duty is to discuss questions of high military policy.

Its members consist of the Secretary and Under-Secretary of State for War (neither of whom have power to vote), the chief of the general staff, and the general officers selected to command armies in war. The following consultative members may be invited to attend :—The inspectors-general of artillery, engineers, cavalry and medical services and the chief of the intendance division of the Staff Corps.

(4) *Central Promotion Committee.*—This consists normally of the chief of the general staff and the army corps commanders who meet annually in the autumn at Rome to consider the claims to promotion of colonels and of general officers. The general commanding the carabinieri and the inspectors-general of artillery, cavalry, engineers and medical services may be called in to give an opinion on officers in their branch of the service.

(5) *The Commandant General of Carabinieri.*
(6) *The Judge Advocate General.*
(7) *The Army Commanders.*
(8) *The Army Corps Commanders.*
(9) The *Inspectorates-General* of cavalry, artillery, mountain troops, engineers, commissariat and medical services.

Local Administration.

The functions of army corps and divisional commanders with reference to administration are not proportionate to the importance of their action as regards command and are limited to general supervision of the interior economy of units. In this duty, the army corps commander is assisted by the medical commissariat and veterinary directors. The intendance division of the staff corps has no active administrative duties in peace time, though it contains the nucleus of the administrative staffs of the larger units which are formed on mobilization.

The actual administrative work is carried on in peace time by the administrative directorates of the War Office in conjunction with local permanent administrative councils.

These permanent administrative councils are established at the depôt of each regiment or of each establishment of similar importance. The greater part of the regiment is usually stationed at the same garrison as the depôt: where this is not the case the permanent council decentralizes some of its powers to a regimental administrative council.

The commanding officer or director is usually president, the commandant of the depôt being the executive member who is responsible for the interior economy of the unit. An accountant officer is usually the secretary.

Demands for pay, stores, clothing, rations, &c., are made through the permanent administrative councils. The monthly pay lists and equipment ledgers are audited by the administrative councils and forwarded to the War Office.

CHAPTER III.

STAFF.

General Officers of the Staff.

In Italy the term "General Officers of the Staff" is applied collectively to the general officers in the army. The most important of these are the chief of the general staff, the generals designated to command armies in war, and the army corps and divisional commanders. The total establishment of the general officers of the staff is as follows :—

    58 Lieutenant-Generals.
    95 Major-Generals.
     4 Inspector-Generals of Military Sanitation.
     1 Inspector-General Commissariat duties.
   ―――
  158

The Staff Corps.

The officers of the Staff Corps assist the chief of the general staff in preparation for war and generally carry out the duties usually known in other countries as "general staff duties."

The establishment of the Staff Corps is as follows :—

    17 Colonels.
     3 Lieutenant-Colonels.
    52 Lieutenant-Colonels or Majors.
    83 Captains.
  ―――
  155

The Functions of the Chief of the General Staff.

The Chief of the Corps of the General Staff must be a full general or lieutenant-general : the post is at present held by General Pollio. The functions of the chief of the general staff and his subordinates include the following :—

1. Advice to the War Minister in questions of military policy.
2. Collaboration with the staffs of allied powers regarding measures necessary for mutual military action.
3. The preparation of war plans, including arrangements for mobilization and concentration.
4. The organization and equipment of the army and its various services.
5. The training and military education of the army and the preparation of training manuals (in consultation with the inspectors-general).
6. The study of the military resources of foreign countries.
7. The organization of frontier and coast defences.
8. Collaboration with the Admiralty as regards the joint action of the naval and military services in war.
9. The conduct of army manœuvres.

In addition the Chief of the General Staff commands the Staff Corps and is, *ipso facto*, a member of all important military committees.

Organization.

The headquarters of the Staff Corps is situated in Rome in the same building as the War Ministry.

The personnel at headquarters is divided into the following divisions and groups :—

(a) *Secretariat and offices directly under the Chief of the General Staff.*—The duty of the cabinet is to collate and co-ordinate the work of the two divisions and to deal with questions affecting the Staff Corps as a whole. It also deals with the Staff College.

The staff consists of—

General Staff.—2 Colonels, 3 Lieutenant-Colonels, 10 Captains.

Probationers ("Applicati di S.M.").—2 Captains.

Attached ("Comandati").—2 Lieut.-Colonels, 2 Majors, 7 Captains.

(b) *The Operations Division* which deals with questions relative to the employment of the army in peace and in war ; the historical section, the Italian attachés to foreign Powers, and the Geographical Institute are auxiliaries of the Operations Division.

Staff (not including 11 Military Attachés).
General Staff.—1 Lieutenant-General, 4 Lieutenant-Colonels, 7 Captains.
Probationers.—9 Captains.
Attached.—1 Lieutenant-Colonel, 15 Captains, 1 Lieutenant, 7 Civilian Draughtsmen.

(c) *The Intendance Division* which is concerned with the study of the working of the various administrative services, and more particularly with problems connected with mobilization and with the movement of troops by sea and land both in peace and war. It is assisted in the latter duty by the *central commission* for the transport of troops by rail and by the *military railway committee* which has branches at Venice, Turin, Ancona and Naples. The central military library and the printing office are under the direct control of the General Staff.

Staff of the Intendance Division.
General Staff.—1 Lieutenant-General, 2 Colonels, 1 Lieutenant-Colonel, 1 Major, 7 Captains.
Probationers.—10 Captains.
Attached.—2 Lieut.-Colonels, 1 Major, 18 Captains, 1 Medical Major, 1 Medical Captain.
Central Library.—1 Lieutenant-Colonel.

In case of war the general in charge of the Operations Division becomes deputy-chief of the staff, and the general in charge of the intendance division becomes intendant-general of the army in the field. A small nucleus of Staff Corps officers remain in Rome to carry out the office work, the remainder are distributed among the headquarter, army and army corps staffs.

The Institute of Military Geography, which is situated in Florence, is controlled by the Chief of the General Staff. The commandant of the Institute is a lieutenant or major-general with a permanent staff of 9 to 12 officers and 96 civilians (draughtsmen, printers, clerks, etc.). The chief executive work is the production of maps and the instruction of attached officers; the theoretical work includes the study of geodesy, topography, triangulation and the development of the means of mechanical reproduction.

Personnel.

The officers of the Staff Corps are recruited from selected Staff College graduates who are attached to the staff as probationers for one year. During the first six months of this period they are attached to the staff at headquarters; during the last six months they are attached to the staff of an army corps or a division. They are then examined by a special commission convened by the Chief of the General Staff after which they are admitted to staff corps appointments in order of seniority, provided they have commanded a unit of their arm for at least two years.

On promotion to major they are sent back to regimental duty for two years, after which they are re-admitted to the staff corps in order of seniority provided their records of service are satisfactory. After promotion to lieutenant-colonel, it is optional whether an officer returns to regimental duty or not, but a colonel on the staff corps is not promoted major-general unless he has commanded a regiment for at least two years. Above the rank of major, staff corps appointments are given by selection and not by seniority.

As will be seen from the above the Staff Corps in Italy is largely a close corporation in which officers may remain for nearly the whole of their service.

In addition to executive work the Staff Corps acts as a centre of instruction for attached probationary officers, who, at the same time relieve them of some of their routine and clerical work. Special courses are also held in foreign languages, railway working and administration and in the study of supplies, which are attended by a proportion of the probationers.

Uniform.

General Officers.—Full dress. Silver epaulettes and lace. Cloak and cape, grey with silver buttons. Tunic—black, double breasted, edged with scarlet, turn-down collar of black velvet with horizontal red lines. Trousers—grey with double red stripe.

Undress. No aiguillette or epaulette. Tunic of similar colour and shape to full dress with no ornament beyond a silver shoulder strap denoting rank. Grey trousers with double scarlet stripe. Forage cap—dark blue with scarlet band embroidered with silver and rows of silver braid denoting rank. Badge—an eagle. On ordinary occasions, a single-breasted black serge jacket is worn instead of the tunic.

Service dress. Forage cap of grey green cloth with peak of same material.

Tunic—Norfolk jacket of grey green cloth with four outside pockets; rolled collar.

Breeches—grey green.

Boots.

Greatcoat—double-breasted long-skirted coat of grey green cloth.

Badges of rank.

In undress, the rank of general officers is denoted by the gold stars on their shoulder straps: one star for a major-general, two stars for a lieutenant-general, three stars for a full general.

On the forage cap, the rank is shown by a corresponding number of narrow rows of lace, sewn above the band of silver embroidery. General officers commanding army corps are distinguished by a gold crown in addition to the stars on the shoulder straps and wear a gold instead of a silver eagle in their forage cap.

In service dress, the badges of rank are the same as in undress uniform.

Officers of the Staff Corps.—Full dress. Gold epaulettes and lace. Cloak and cape—blue with velvet collar. Tunic—black with blue velvet collar. Trousers—black with double gold stripe divided by blue piping.

Undress, same as above without aiguillette or epaulettes. Forage cap with band of dark blue velvet.

Brigade majors wear their regimental uniform with a distinctive star on the sleeve.

Service dress. The same as that worn by general officers.

Badges of ranks.

Rank is denoted by concentric rings of lace on the forage cap, and in undress by stars on the shoulder strap.

Rank.	Stars.	Rings.
Lieutenant	2	2
Captain	3	3
Major	1	One narrow, one broad.
Lieut.-Colonel	2	Two narrow, one broad.
Colonel	3	Three narrow, one broad.

Field officers have their shoulder straps edged with gold or silver lace.

In service dress, the badges of rank are unaltered.

CHAPTER IV.

ORGANIZATION AND MOBILIZATION.
Peace.

The Units of the Active Army.

The active army, when the decree of 17th July, 1910, has been carried out, will consist of the following. A few of the units mentioned are not yet formed :—

- 11 Legions of Carabinieri.
- 1 Recruit Legion of Carabinieri.
- 96 Regiments of Infantry.
- 12 Regiments of Bersaglieri.
- 8 Regiments of "Alpini."
- 29 Regiments of Cavalry.
- 36 Field Artillery Regiments.
- 36 Transport Companies, Field Artillery.
- 1 Horse Artillery Regiment.
- 4 Companies Transport, Horse Artillery.
- 2 Heavy Field Artillery Regiments.
- 2 Mountain Artillery Regiments.
- 10 Regiments Fortress Artillery.
- 6 Regiments of Engineers.
- 1 Specialisti Battalion Engineers.
- 12 Sanitary Companies.
- 12 Commissariat Companies.

The above troops are organized in 12 army corps, to each of which is allotted a territorial limit of command. Each army corps command contains two divisional commanders. The only exception to this is the 9th Army Corps command, which includes the 25th (Sardinian) division in addition to the 17th and 18th divisions.

Each army corps consists of two divisions and corps troops, each division of two infantry brigades and divisional troops.

Incorporated in the army corps commands are eight cavalry brigades, six of which are organised in peace into three cavalry divisions (each of two brigades of two regiments with divisional troops), and three brigades of "Alpini."

For details *see* Appendices II, III, VI, and map.

Army Commander.—In war, the Italian forces would be organized in four armies. The army commanders are designated in peace time, but their duties are confined to the inspecting and supervision of the group of corps which they would command in war. They also carry out any special missions that may be intrusted to them by the Minister for War.

Headquarters are at Genoa, Verona, Milan, and Naples respectively. The peace staff of an army commander designate at present consists of four field officers of the staff, four other officers attached, and four orderly officers.

Army Corps Commander.—The army corps commander (a lieutenant-general) exercises direct control over all troops within the limits of his command and is responsible for their general efficiency. The technical training of the cavalry, artillery, engineers and medical service is under the inspectors-general of those arms.

The army corps staff consists of one colonel, one lieutenant-colonel, one captain, two attached captains, a veterinary officer, a transport officer, and an orderly officer.

The army corps commander decentralizes some of his authority to the artillery and engineer commands, and is further assisted by directors of the medical, commissariat and veterinary services. These directors act as technical advisers to the army corps commander and are responsible for the proper working of their departments.

Cavalry Divisional Commander.—This officer is a lieutenant-general or major-general, and is responsible to the inspector-general of cavalry for the technical training of the cavalry and to the army corps commander for mobilization arrangements and discipline. His staff consists of one colonel and one captain.

Infantry Divisional Commander.—The commander of an infantry division (a lieutenant-general) is responsible to the army corps commander for the mobilization arrangements, discipline and training of the troops under his command. His staff consists of one lieutenant-colonel on the staff, one or two staff captains, two or three attached staff captains and an orderly officer.

Infantry and Cavalry Brigade Commanders.—Brigade commanders are directly responsible to their divisional generals for the drill, discipline and general efficiency of their commands.

In the case of cavalry brigades not allotted to cavalry divisions, the brigade commander acts more as an inspecting officer than as tactical commander.

Brigadiers are assisted by a staff of one brigade major and an orderly officer.

Field Artillery Commands.—Three new field artillery commands were instituted in 1910. The present organization consists of nine commands in all, distributed as follows :—

Field Artillery Command.	Army Corps Region.
(1) Turin	I.
(2) Alessandria	II (less the 6th Regiment).
(3) Milan	III (plus the 6th Regiment).
(4) Cremona	IV.
(5) Verona	V.
(6) Bologna	VI and VII.
(7) Florence	VIII.
(8) Rome	IX.
(9) Naples	X, XI, XII.

Each command is under a major-general with a staff of two or three officers. The commandant supervises the horse, field and mountain artillery in one or more army corps regions, and is responsible to the inspector-general of artillery for technical instruction and administrative services, and to the divisional commander for discipline, mobilization and tactical instruction as regards co-operation with the other arms.

Fortress Artillery Commander.—The functions of the commandants of fortress artillery are generally on the same system as those of the field artillery. A redistribution of the territorial limits of the fortress artillery commands was made in 1910, when an additional command was established at Mantua.

Command headquarters are now situated at Genoa, Mantua, Rome and Piacenza.

Artillery Directions.—Each artillery command has under its control from one to three directions, each under a field officer. The duty of these directions is to take charge of all artillery material and stores not in the possession of units and to carry out repairs.

The total personnel so employed amounts to about 85 officers and 500 men, many of the latter being civilians.

Engineer Commands.—Engineer commands are five in number, distributed as follows :—

	Headquarters.	Army Corps Region.
No. I	Turin	Nos. I. II, IV.
„ II	Verona	„ III, V.
„ III	Bologna	„ VI, VII.
„ IV	Rome	„ VIII, IX.
„ V	Naples	„ X, XI, XII.

Each engineer commandant (a major-general) has charge of the engineer services in the corresponding army corps regions. His duties are analagous to those of a commandant of artillery.

Engineer Directions.—There are 12 engineer directions (each under a colonel or lieut.-colonel). They are responsible to the engineer commands for the maintenance of all military buildings and works, and for the carrying out of new constructions.

Commissariat Directions.

There are 12 commissariat directions, one to each army corps region. The director is responsible to the army corps commander for the proper working of the service and for preparations for mobilization, and to the Minister for War for general administration, and contracts for supplies and stores.

Medical directions.—There are 12 medical directions, one to each army corps. The functions of these directions are analagous to those of the commissariat directions.

Inspectors-General.

(a) *Cavalry.*—The inspector-general is a lieutenant-general with headquarters at Rome. He is responsible for the technical training of cavalry, including the courses at the cavalry school, and for the administration and management of the remount depôts. Under the authority of the War Minister, he makes periodical inspections of the different regiments and establishments.

His staff consists of one colonel or lieutenant-colonel, one field officer and two captains.

(b) *Artillery.*—1. The inspector-general of artillery is a lieutenant-general resident in Rome; he is under the orders of the Minister for War.

The following are the more important functions of the inspector-general and his staff :—

   (i) Confidential advice to the War Minister on any point affecting artillery from the technical or organic point of view.

  (ii) Collaboration with the chief of the staff on the organization or mobilization of the arm, or on the armament of fortifications.

 (iii) Collaboration with the inspector-general of engineers on points affecting their respective arms; a technical commission composed of the artillery and engineer inspectors can be convened if necessary.

 (iv) The direction of researches and experiments regarding artillery in conjunction with the directorate of experiments.

Until the year 1910, the duty of inspecting field, mountain and fortress artillery, was deputed to the inspectors-general of field artillery and fortress artillery respectively. This duty is now carried out direct by the staff of the inspector-general.

2. The Inspectorate of Artillery Construction.

This inspectorate does not form an integral part of the inspectorate-general, but is independent of it.

The inspector is a lieutenant-general or major-general with a staff of 5 officers, 8 attached officers and 17 subordinates. He is an *ex-officio* member of the permanent artillery committee and is responsible for all matters connected with the manufacture of artillery, and for the economical working of the Government arsenals.

(c) *Mountain Troops.*—The inspector-general of mountain troops is responsible for the special training of the "alpini" and of the mountain artillery. Headquarters are at Rome; the staff consists of one major, one captain and one lieutenant.

(d) *Engineers.*—The inspector-general of engineers whose headquarters are at Rome carries out duties generally analogous to those of the inspector-general of artillery. The inspectorate is especially charged with the discussion of plans for permanent fortifications. It is divided into an inspectorate of engineer troops and an inspectorate of engineer "constructions."

Staff.

1 Inspector lieutenant-general.
2 Lieutenant or major-generals.
1 Colonel or lieutenant-colonel.
2 Lieutenant-colonels or majors.
6 Captains.
25 Subordinates.

(e) *Medical Services.*—The inspector-general is a surgeon-lieutenant-general with headquarters at Rome. He is assisted by three surgeon major-generals and five additional medical officers. The inspectorate carries out such inspections of hospitals and medical institutions as the Minister for War may direct, and acts as a consultative expert body on subjects connected with the army medical service, sanitation or hygiene.

(f) *Commissariat Services.*—The inspector is styled Major-General Inspector of Commissariat Services. He is the permanent inspector of the administrative services and especially of the commissariat. He is the assistant of the War Minister and of the Army Intendants. He directs the preparation for war of the commissariat services and with this object he draws up the necessary statistics that may be necessary in war. On mobilization he is responsible for the exploitation of the resources of the theatre of war.

(g) *The Directorate of Experiments of Artillery.*—This directorate is located at Turin and has the use of the experimental ground at Cirie. It is under the command of a Director (Colonel, Lieutenant-Colonel or Major), who has a staff of twelve officers. This directorate is a dependency of the inspectorate-general of artillery, though considerable latitude is allowed in the matter of experiments.

Military Districts.

Organization.—(*See* Appendix III.)—Italy is divided into 88 military districts, distributed in proportion to the density of the population and coinciding with the administrative sub-divisions of the country. Six of these districts are looked upon as double so that there may be said to be 94 districts in all, coinciding with the 94 regiments of the line. Districts bear the name of the town in which their headquarters is situated and are divided into two classes. The 1st class districts, 25 in number, have their offices in the same town as the headquarters of the military divisions. The 63 2nd class districts form detachments from the 1st class districts.

Personnel.—The following is the total establishment of personnel :—

Lt.-Colonels or Majors.	Captains.	Accountant Officers.		Under Officers.	Clerks.
		Captains.	Other Ranks.		
88	176	25	130	394	329

Duties.—The following are the duties carried out by the staff of military districts :—

(1) The organization of the recruiting service.

(2) The requisition of animals and vehicles, namely in peace the preparation of lists of the animals and vehicles available : in war the actual requisitioning of those required for military service. The staffs of the district is assisted in this duty by requisitioning commissions.

(3) The administration of the mobile and territorial militia.

(4) The arrangements for calling up reservists for training.

(5) The payment of retired officers or of reserve officers.

(6) The fabrication of certain articles of clothing.

Mobile Militia.—The mobile militia consists of four annual classes of men between the ages of 29 and 32, most of whom have served their full term of service, and all of whom have received some military training. The machinery for the following units exist in peace time though the men are not embodied :—

51 regiments* of infantry (each of 3 battalions of
   4 companies).
20 battalions of bersaglieri (4 companies).
38 companies of "alpini."
31 squadrons of cavalry.
78 batteries of field and mountain artillery.
78 companies of fortress artillery.
24 companies of artillery train.
58 companies of engineers.
4 companies of engineers train.

The total strength of the mobile militia that could be mobilized probably does not exceed 200,000 men.

Territorial Militia.—Organization exist in time of peace for the formation of the following units on mobilization :—

324 battalions of infantry (4 companies each).
22 battalions of "alpini" (75 companies)
100 companies of fortress artillery.
30 companies of engineers.

The total strength of the territorial militia is rather over 2,000,000 men, but only 400,000 of these are trained.

War.

Subdivision of Forces.—On the outbreak of war, the military forces are divided into field troops and garrison troops.

The former category includes the whole of the active army (except the fortress artillery), the greater part of the mobile militia, and the "alpini" of the territorial militia.

The garrison troops are formed of the fortress artillery, the mobile militia that are not required for the field armies, and the territorial militia.

The field troops would be formed into four armies, the whole under the supreme command of the King, with the Chief of the General Staff as chief of the staff, and the head of the intendance division of the staff corps as intendant-general. Each army would comprise three army corps, one cavalry division and army troops.

---

* 3 regiments of mobile militia belong to Sardinia and 48 regiments correspond with the 48 brigades of the regular army. The 2 regiments of each brigade of infantry of the line are in possession of clothing, arms, and equipment for 1 regiment of mobile militia.

The Staff of an Army.
General staff.
   1 major-general ; chief of the staff.
   1 colonel.
   1 major.
   3 staff captains.
   3 aides-de-camp.

Intendance.
   1 major-general ; army intendant.
   1 colonel : chief of the intendant staff.
   2 staff captains.
   1 aide-de-camp.

An army consists approximately of :—
   3 to 4 army corps.
   1 cavalry division, and the following army troops :—
   1 detachment heavy artillery.
   2 bridging trains.
   1 telegraph company.
   1 balloon park.
   1 electric light park.
   1 artillery park.
   1 engineer park.
  15 field hospitals.
   1 advanced depôt medical material.
   1 field bakery.
   1 subsistence park.
   1 clothing depôt.
   1 remount depôt.

Army Corps.—The staff consists of staff officers, artillery and engineer commandants, directors of medical service and commissariat.

The component parts of an army corps are :—
        2 infantry divisions (active army).
        1   „   „ (mobile militia).

Corps troops ... {
 1 regiment of bersaglieri.
 1   „   of cavalry.
 1   „   of field artillery (containing two groups each of 3 batteries).
 1 telegraph company and park.

Columns and parks
{ 1 corps artillery park.
1 ,, ammunition column.
1 ,, engineer park.
1 section.
1 supply ambulance.
4 field hospitals.
1 supply column.
1 reserve supply park. } For corps troops.

Approximate strength—50,000 men, 8,400 horses, 126 guns.

Cavalry Division.—The staff consists of officers of the staff corps, medical and commissariat services.

Troops...
{ 2 brigades of cavalry of 2 regiments each (20 squadrons in all).
1 group of horse artillery (2 batteries).
1 bersaglieri cyclist battalion.
1 cavalry ambulance.
1 supply section.
1 bridging section (44 yards bridge).
Divisional ammunition column.

Approximate strength—4,200 men, 4,200 horses, 8 guns.

Infantry Division.—The staff is composed of staff corps officers and representatives of the medical and commissariat services.

Active army ...
{ 2 infantry brigades, each of 2 regiments (12 battalions in all).
1 regiment of field artillery (containing 2 groups, one of 2 and one of 3 batteries).
1 company of engineers.
1 bridging section (44 yards bridge).
Telephone park with 25 miles of line and 16 stations.
Divisional ammunition column.
Field ambulance.
Supply section.

Mobile militia ... As above, with the addition of 2 or 3 squadrons of cavalry and 1 or 2 battalions of bersaglieri.

Approximate strength—14,200 men, 1,400 horses, 30 guns.

Mountain Troops.—The mountain troops, whose function in war will be to cover the mobilization and concentration of the main armies, comprise the following units :—

3 brigades (26 battalions) of "alpini" of the active army, reinforced by 38 companies of mobile militia.
75 companies of "alpini" territorial militia.
2 regiments (24 batteries) of mountain artillery.
15 batteries of mobile militia.

A *Mountain Brigade* consists of—
5 or more battalions "alpini."
2 or more mountain batteries.
1 detachment mountain transport.
2 field hospitals (50 beds each).
1 mountain ambulance.
1 mountain ammunition column.
1 section pioneers.
1 reserve supply column.

The remaining troops consist of the 25th (Sardinian) division (should it not be incorporated in the 9th Army Corps), 1 infantry brigade of carabinieri, (2 regiments each of 3 battalions), 2 squadrons of mounted carabinieri, 23 battalions of custom house guards, a proportion of the mobile militia, the whole of the territorial militia (except the "alpini" units) and the fortress artillery.

NOTE.—The divisions at Bari and at Cagliari only consist of 1 brigade each in peace time.

Mobilization.

Preparation of Mobilization Scheme.—The following documents are prepared in peace time under the authority of the Chief of the General Staff, and are circulated confidentially to all the higher military authorities :—

(*a*) Order of battle and places of concentration of the army.

(*b*) Orders as to movements of troops and railway timetables.

(*c*) Tables establishing the localities where the larger units are to be quartered.

(*d*) Mobilization gazette containing details of all appointments other than those held by officers in peace time and allotting complement and reserve officers to units.

On the instructions contained in the above documents, commanding officers and heads of departments draw up schemes for the mobilization of their respective units. These schemes are produced at all inspections. All vehicles and harness in the possession of units must be tested annually to insure that they are in serviceable condition.

System of Mobilization.—Speaking generally the mobilization of the army is carried out on the "regional" principle, that is to say the reservists required to complete a unit to war strength are furnished by the districts close to the peace station of the unit concerned; this principle does not apply to the grenadier regiments or to the engineers who draw their reservists from the whole of Italy.

Each depôt of infantry, cavalry, artillery and engineers, has in its charge the mobilization clothing and equipment of the unit concerned and of a corresponding unit of mobile militia. The reservists either join the depôt direct and are there equipped and armed, or, if they reside at a distance from their depôts, they report themselves to the headquarters of their recruiting district and are thence forwarded to the depôt. When the units are equipped they leave for the places of concentration.

The territorial militia are mobilized in the military districts, certain districts being specially told off for the formation of artillery and engineer units. The territorial militia are not mobilized simultaneously but in three successive echelons.

The Rate of Mobilization.—The first day of mobilization is reckoned to be the day after the issue of the order to mobilize.

Particulars as to the time necessary for mobilization are kept secret. The following facts may, however, be assumed to be approximately correct.

Cavalry.—The peace establishment is higher than the war establishment, and a cavalry regiment can consequently mobilize in 24 hours: the process has been performed experimentally in three hours.

Mountain Troops.—The "alpini" and the mountain artillery can mobilize at a more rapid rate than other units. As regards the "alpini," the battalion staff, the men on the peace establishment, and the first echelon of the convoy would be ready to march a few hours after the receipt of the order to mobilize. Units would be reached by the reservists of the active army and by the 2nd and 3rd echelons of the convoy at the end of the 3rd day. The companies of mobile militia would be at their war stations before the 8th day, and the territorial militia would be ready to march on the morning of the 8th day. The mountain artillery could mobilize at about the same rate.

Infantry of the Line.—The rate of mobilization varies according to local circumstances. Units favourably situated would be ready to move by the evening of the 3rd day; in a considerable number of cases, however, mobilization would not be completed until the morning of the 5th day.

Artillery.—Until the reorganization of the artillery is completed, it is difficult to fix even an approximate period for the completion of mobilization. Probably the artillery would complete mobilization between the 7th and 11th days.

Engineers.

Mobilization would be completed between the 7th and the 11th day.

CHAPTER V.
OFFICERS AND NON-COMMISSIONED OFFICERS.

The various ranks of officers are sub-lieutenant, lieutenant, captain, major, lieutenant-colonel, colonel, major-general, lieutenant-general, and general (only given as a rule when a lieutenant-general is appointed to command an army in the field).

Officers of the Active Army.

The various categories of officers are :—
1. In active employment.
2. At disposal ("disponibilita"). This position is equivalent to temporary unemployment on full pay. It is usually only applicable to general officers or staff officers of the higher ranks, who have been placed at disposal for administrative reasons. Cases have occurred, however, of officers having been placed at disposal as a disciplinary measure.
3. Awaiting employment ("aspettativa"). This corresponds to our half-pay (the rate is usually $\frac{3}{5}$ of full pay). The usual reasons for being placed on half pay are :—
    (a) Abolition of appointment.
    (b) Reduction of establishment.
    (c) Temporary physical unfitness.
    (d) As a punishment.

Officers are recruited from : —

(a) Students who have completed the course at the military educational establishments at Modena or Turin.

(b) Under officers with at least 4 years' service, who have passed through the under officers' course at Modena. 25 per cent. of the commissions vacant are allotted to under officers.

(c) Complement officers with 6 months' service in that capacity, who have the requisite educational qualifications.

The age of candidates for first commission is between the ages of 19 and 28.

Promotion is carried out on a general list for each branch of the service. The appointment and promotion of general officers is nominally by selection, but it is very seldom that a general staff officer who has commanded a regiment for the prescribed period is not promoted; that of other officers partly by selection, partly by seniority. For promotion of staff officers *see* page 31.

Age of Retirement of Officers.—Officers of the active army are retired or placed in auxiliary position on attaining the following age limits :—

	Combatant Branches.	Non-combatant Branches.
Lieutenant-General	65	—
Major-General	62	65
Colonel	58	62
Lieutenant-Colonel	56	58
Major	53	56
Captain	50	53
Lieutenant } Sub-Lieutenant	48	50

Reserve of Officers.

Reserve officers are called officers on furlough ("ufficiali in congedo") and are divided into five categories :—

1. On temporary furlough ("congedo provvisorio"). Officers considered unfit for further promotion through no special fault may be sent on temporary furlough on three-fifths pay until qualified for retired pay.
2. In auxiliary position ("posizione ausilaria"). This class consists of officers who have attained the age limit but are considered to be still capable of employment on mobilization. Their rate of retired pay is slightly increased.
3. Reserve officers. Pensioned or discharged officers still capable of performing sedentary work.
4. Complement officers. This class, which numbers over 13,000, consists of under officers and soldiers who have completed their term of service in the active army and have passed through the student officers class, of qualified military students who have not been successful in passing into the army but qualified in military subjects, and of officers who have retired but are still under 40 years of age.
5. Officers of the territorial militia. Persons of suitable position and education may become officers of the territorial militia on serving for a month with a

regular unit. Under officers of over eight years' service, who no longer belong to the active army or mobile militia, may be granted commissions regardless of other conditions.

Non-Commissioned Officers.

N.C.Os. consist of lance-corporals, corporals, corporal-majors, and under-officers. The latter form a class between the officers and the rank and file of the army and are serjeants, serjeant-majors, and warrant officers (marescialli). Warrant officers have 3 ranks—marshals, chief marshals, and marshal-majors—corresponding with colour-serjeants, battalion, and regimental serjeant-majors.

Promotion of N.C.Os.—Army corps commanders appoint warrant officers, and commanders of units the remaining ranks. Lance-corporals are appointed after 12 months' service, corporals from lance-corporals, and corporal-majors from corporals with 6 and 3 months' service in these ranks respectively.

Serjeants are selected from corporal-majors, or corporals, from volunteers of 15 months' service who have extended their service to 3 years with the colours, and from those who have passed a course for recruit-serjeants, open to 1-year volunteers, students, and corporal-majors, corporals, and men of the regular army who fulfil certain conditions.

Promotion to the rank of serjeant-major is by selection from serjeants with 3 years' service who have passed the prescribed examination. Promotion to higher ranks is by seniority, and in all cases under officers not considered fit for promotion are sent to the reserve.

Privileges of N.C.Os.—Serjeants after 3 years' service and serjeant-majors after 4 years' service in that rank who re-engage receive a bounty of £40, and all under-officers serving for 3 years have the right of a brother being placed in the 2nd category instead of the 1st category.

After 13 years' service under-officers can apply for employment in the ordnance department, etc., or in any Government department, or on the railways, one-third of the posts in these being reserved for ex-soldiers.

Retirement.—Under-officers may retire after 20 and must retire after 30 years' service.

(For pay, etc., *see* Chapter XVII).

CHAPTER VI.

CARABINIERI REALI.

The Carabinieri are an organization somewhat similar to the French gendarmerie.

They are under the War Office as regards organization, discipline, administration and instruction, under the Admiralty as regards duties in naval arsenals, or in connection with the personnel of the Navy and under the Ministry of the Interior as regards police duties.

Peace.

Organization.—The following is the organization of the Carabinieri :—

    (1) Headquarter Staff.
    (2) Eleven territorial legions.
    (3) One recruit legion.

Headquarter Staff—

  1 Lieutenant-General (Commandant).
  2 Major-Generals (inspecting officers).
  1 Colonel or Lieutenant-Colonel.
  3 Captains.
  3 Lieutenants.
14 Non-Commissioned Officers and men.

Headquarters are situated at Rome. The Commandant carries out the directions of the Ministers for War and for the Interior and he is responsible for the administration of the corps as a whole, including all questions of promotion.

The Territorial Legions.—The eleven territorial legions are distributed throughout Italy. Each legion is divided into one or more divisions; each division into one or more companies.

The Rome legion furnishes the special squadron of 4 officers and 80 men, which forms the King's Bodyguard.

Carabinieri undergo some military instruction annually, including target practice. The dismounted men are each provided with a folding bicycle, Costa type.

The total establishment of the territorial legions is as follows:—

Colonels commanding Legions	11
Field Officers commanding Divisions	67
King's Squadron	1
Captains	200
Lieutenants	237
Sub-Lieutenants	119
Medical Officers	4
Administrative Officers	33
Veterinary Officers	7
Total Officers	679*

	Mounted.	Dismounted.
Non-commissioned officers (including lance-corporals)	1,106	6,585
"Carabinieri"	2,345	17,770
Total non-commissioned officers and men	3,451	24,355
Horses	3,451	—

Recruits, all of whom are volunteers, are drawn either from the recruit contingents of the regular army or from soldiers actually serving. Service is for three years, nine months of which is spent with the recruit legion, where a regular course of military instruction is gone through, similar to that carried out in the regular infantry or cavalry.

---

* The following officers have been added by orders dated 9th December, 1911, but no details have been received:—
        1 Lieutenant-Colonel.
        1 Major.
        6 Captains.
        6 Lieutenants.
        6 2nd Lieutenants.

The standard of height is 5 ft. 5 in. for dismounted and 5 ft. 6 in. for mounted men.

The Recruit Legion.—The recruit legion is a corps of instruction consisting of :—

> Headquarters.
> 6 companies.
> 1 squadron.
> 2 depôts.

Establishment of Recruit Legion.

	Officers.				
	Headquarters.	6 Companies.	1 Squadron.	Depôt Companies.	Total.
Commandant	1	—	—	—	—
Lieutenant-Colonel or Major	2	—	—	—	—
Captain	1	.6	1	1	—
Lieutenants	1	13	3	2	—
Sub-Lieutenants	—	5	1	2	—
Medical Officers :—					
Captain	1	—	—	—	—
Lieutenant or 2nd Lieutenant	1	—	—	—	—
Lieutenant-Colonel or Major i/c Administration	1	—	—	—	—
Captain do. do.	1	—	—	—	—
Lieutenant or 2nd Lieutenant	1	—	—	—	—
Veterinary Captain	1	—	—	—	—
Bandmaster	1	—	—	—	—
Total	12	24	5	5	46

Non-Commissioned Officers and Rank and File.

	Headquarters.		6 Companies.	1 Squadron.	Depôt Cagliari.		Depôt Palermo.	
	Mtd.	Dis.			Mtd.	Dis.	Mtd.	Dis.
N.C.Os.	1	78	139	47	7	8	7	26
Recruits	—	—	1,400	198	50	50	50	200
Total	1	78	1,539	245	57	58	57	226
Horses	—	—	—	199	37	—	32	—

War Organization.—The Carabinieri in addition to their police duties furnish the following contingents, which are at the disposal of the Commander-in-Chief :—

1 brigade of dismounted men (2 regiments, each of 3 battalions).
1 mounted division (2 squadrons).

These are entirely composed of men serving with the colours ; the squadrons and battalions are of about the same strength as similar units in the infantry or artillery.
In addition they provided the following units :—

Commander-in-Chief's headquarters... 2 special sections.
Headquarters of each army ... ... 1 special section.
The General Intendance ... ... 2 ordinary sections.
The Intendance of each army ... 2 ,, ,,
Headquarters of each army corps ... 1 ordinary section.
Headquarters of each division ... 1 ,, ,,
Headquarters of each cavalry division 1 ,, ,,

A special section consists of 1 officer, 56 men, 30 horses and 1 cart. An ordinary section of 1 officer, 49 men, 30 horses and 1 cart.

Uniform.

The King's Bodyguard.

Full Dress.—Helmet of white metal with brass ornaments and crest, long black horsehair mane, scarlet and white plume.

Steel cuirass.

Tunic : dark blue double-breasted, white aiguillettes and epaulettes.

White buckskin breeches, white gloves.

Long jack-boots.

Undress.—Head-dress : cap with crowned eagle as a badge.

Tunic : dark blue, double-breasted, red piping.

Trousers : dark blue, double scarlet stripe if dismounted, grey with double black stripe if mounted.

White belt with pouch.

Cloak : dark blue with cape ; scarlet lining.

The Carabinieri.—Head-dress : black felt cocked hat with silver badge, in full dress a scarlet and blue plume.

Tunic : dark blue, double-breasted ; in full dress white aiguillettes and epaulettes.

Great coat : dark blue.

Trousers, cloak and belt the same as the undress uniform of the King's Bodyguard.

At night, or when on a bicycle or in fatigue dress a cap is worn instead of a cocked hat, the badge being a flaming grenade with the royal cipher.

Armament and Equipment.

Officers and serjeants, sword and revolver. Other ranks : carbine 1891 pattern, revolver and sword. Equipment as for infantry or cavalry ; the straps are of buff leather, pipeclayed.

Ammunition.

In peace time men carry 36 rounds of both revolver and carbine ammunition, 18 of the latter being buckshot.

Cyclists carry the carbine slung on the back and the revolver on the left side of the belt.

Non-Commissioned Officers.

The various ranks of under-officers are lance-serjeant, serjeant, billeting marshal, chief billeting marshal, and billeting marshal major.

Lance-serjeants are selected from lance-corporals and "carabinieri," serjeants from lance-serjeants with 2 years' service, and billeting marshals from serjeants with 4 years' service in that rank. After 4 years' service in their ranks billeting and chief billeting marshals are promoted.

One-third of the under-officers are promoted by selection and two-thirds by seniority.

N.C.Os. may retire after 20 years' service, and must retire after 30 years' service.

General Remarks.

Although the Carabinieri have a total peace establishment of about 33,000, no difficulty has been found in maintaining the strength of the corps.

The men are highly respected and looked up to, especially in remote country districts.

CHAPTER VII.

INFANTRY.

The infantry comprises the infantry of the line, bersaglieri. alpine regiments ("alpini") and the discipline companies.

Organization.

Infantry of the Line.—The infantry of the line consists of 2 regiments of grenadiers and 94 regiments of the line.

The regiments are composed for the most part of 3 four-company battalions, a machine gun section,* and a depôt for the regiment and for the mobile militia. The grenadier regiments, however, have no depôts for mobile militia.

The regiment stationed at Cagliari in Sardinia has a cyclist company.

The following 24 regiments have had a fourth battalion added by Royal Decrees of 7th December, 1911, and 27th June, 1912 :—

4th, 6th, 7th, 18th, 20th, 22nd, 23rd, 26th, 30th, 34th, 35th, 37th, 40th, 50th, 52nd, 57th, 60th, 63rd, 68th, 79th, 82nd, 84th, 89th, 93rd.

These units will probably be used as part of the new colonial army and will not alter the composition of the regiments in Italy.

The 96 regiments are organized in 48 brigades. The 1st brigade is called "The Grenadiers of Sardinia," the 2nd "The King's," the 6th "The Queen's," the remainder are named after towns and provinces ; these titles, however, have no territorial meaning. The line regiments are numbered from 1 to 94. The names and compositions of the 48 brigades and their distinguishing colours are contained in Appendix I.

Each brigade has a corresponding regiment of mobile militia ; on mobilization each depôt organizes one-half of its linked mobile militia regiment.

---

* *See* Chap. XI.

The peace establishment of a grenadier or infantry regiment is as follows:—

Officers.	Headquarters.	12 Companies.	Machine Gun Section.	Nucleus Milizia Mobile.	Depôt.	Total Regiment.	Cycle Company, Sardinia.	Total, 96 Regts. and 1 Company Cyclists of Sardinia.
Commandant Colonel	1	—	—	—	—	1	—	96
Lieut. - Colonel or Major	—	—	—	—	1	1	—	96
Lieut. - Colonel or Major	3	—	—	—	—	3	—	312
,, a dispozione and M.M.	1	—	—	1	—	2	—	192
Captains	2-3	12	—	3	1	18-19	1	1,872
Lieutenants or 2/Lieutenants	3	29	1	3	—	36	3	3,648
Med. Officer Captain	1	—	—	—	—	1	—	96
Med. Officer Captain, Lieutenant or 2/Lieutenant	1	—	—	—	—	1	—	96
Bandmaster	1	—	—	—	—	1	—	96
Total	13-14	41	1	7	2	64-65	4	6,504*
Attached Administration	—	—	—	—	1†	—	—	96
	—	—	—	—	2‡	—	—	192

* The newly-formed 4th battalions have 1 lieutenant-colonel or major, 4 captains and 8 subalterns per battalion.
† Attached for administration.
‡ In charge of magazines and stores.

Non-Commissioned Ranks and Private Soldiers.

	Headquarters.	12 Companies.	M.G. Section.	Mobile Militia.	Depôt.	Total.	Cycle Coy. Sardinia.	Grand Total, 96 Regts. and 1 Coy. Cyclists.
N.C.Os. ...	43*	156	3	12	12	226	17	—
Privates ...	31*	924	11	78	17	1,061	73	—
Horses ...	(3)	—	(4)	—	—	—	—	—
Total ...	74	1,080	17	90	29	1,287	90	132,856†

Details of Non-Commissioned Officers, &c., of a Company and a Machine Gun Section.

A Company.								
S. Major ...	1	—	—	—	—	—	—	—
S. Major or Sjt.	2	—	—	—	—	—	—	—
Corp. Maj. ...	3	—	—	—	—	—	—	—
Corp. Clerk ...	1	—	—	—	—	—	—	—
Corporals ...	6	—	—	—	—	—	—	—
Pioneers ...	4	—	—	—	—	—	—	—
A Machine Gun Section.								
S. Major ...	1	—	—	—	—	—	—	—
S. Major or Sjt.	1	—	—	—	—	—	—	—
Corp. Maj. ...	1	—	—	—	—	—	—	—
Trumpeter ...	1	—	—	—	—	—	—	—

* Includes Band and Armourers, &c.
† 96 companies belonging to the 24 new battalions are included.

Infantry regiments are supposed to change quarters once in every four years in order that the sentiment in the army should be a national one, rather than a local one ; this regulation is not very vigorously enforced. When a regiment changes quarters the depôt is not moved, the depôt personnel and stores being transferred to the incoming regiment.

Peace Establishment.

Infantry and Grenadier Units.

The establishment of infantry units on a peace footing is as follows :—

—	Officers.	Rank and File.	Machine Gun Section.
Company	3 to 4	90	O. R. & F. 1 14
Battalion	13 to 15	374	
Depôt	5	29	
Depôt for Mobile Militia ...	7	90	
Regiment, including Depôt, Depôt for Mobile Militia, Headquarters, Band, &c.	68*	1,287	

* Including 3 attached Administrative Officers.

The peace strength varies considerably according to the time of year ; during the winter months infantry units are below their strength ; during the summer, when reservists are out for training they exceed it. The average strength of a company is about 75 men.

War Establishment.

	Officers.	Rank and File.	Horses.	Vehicles.
Company ...	5	250	1	—
Battalion ...	24	1,019	15	5
Regiment ...	78	3,113	63	18

Bersaglieri.

The Bersaglieri consist of 12 regiments of light infantry, recruited from selected men of good physique. Each regiment except the 4th, 8th and 11th consists of 3 infantry battalions, 1 cyclist battalion and a depôt, each infantry and cyclist battalion of 3 companies. The 4th, 8th and 11th Regiments have 4 battalions. The distribution of infantry battalions to regiments, which is irregular as far as numbers are concerned, is shown by the following table :—

1st Regiment	...	Nos.	1, 7, 9	Battalions.
2nd ,,	...	,,	2, 4, 17	,,
3rd ,,	...	,,	18, 20, 25	,,
4th ,,	...	,,	26, 29, 31, 37	,,
5th ,,	...	,,	14, 22, 24	,,
6th ,,	...	,,	6, 13, 19	,,
7th ,,	...	,,	8, 10, 11	,,
8th ,,	...	,,	3, 5, 12, 38	,,
9th ,,	...	,,	28, 30, 32	,,
10th ,,	...	,,	16, 34, 35	,,
11th ,,	...	,,	15, 27, 33, 39	,,
12th ,,	...	,,	21, 23, 36	,,

The new battalions were formed by Royal Decrees of 7th December, 1911 and 27th June, 1912, and each consists of 1 lieutenant-colonel or major, 3 captains, 6 subalterns, and 3 companies of 90 rank and file. They will probably form part of the new colonial army.

Peace Establishment of Bersaglieri.

—	Headquarters.	Battalion Staff.	Cyclist Battalion. 3 Companies.	9 Companies.	M. G. Section.*	Depôt.†
Colonel	1	—	—	—	—	—
Lieutenant-Colonel or Major	—	—	—	—	—	1
Lieutenant-Colonels or Majors Commanding Battalions	3	1	—	—	—	—
Lieutenant-Colonel or Major not specially detailed	1	—	—	—	—	—
Captains	4	—	3	9	—	1
Lieutenants or 2nd Lieutenants	3	2	9	21	1	—
Medical Officers	2	—	—	—	—	—
	14	3	12	30	1	2
N.C.Os.	22	13	51	117	3	12
Buglers, Pioneers, Privates	5	—	219	693	11	17

* See Chap. XI.
† Each depôt has also two officers who carry out administrative duties.

Total.—12 Regiments—774 officers, 24 officers for administrative duties, 14,766 other ranks.

NOTE.—Cyclist battalions have 1 additional subaltern in charge of the material of the battalion; in other respects their organization is identical with that of the infantry battalions.

Bersaglieri regiments change garrisons periodically, one regiment being stationed in each army corps region. Their system of recruiting is territorial, their system of mobilization is regional.

‡ *Alpine Infantry ("Alpini").*

The "Alpini" regiments consist of eight regiments, divided into 26 battalions, 78 companies, 26 machine gun sections,§

‡ For distribution *see* Appendix II.
§ *See* Chap. XI.

26 nuclei for mobile milizia (one for each battalion) and eight depôts.

Each regiment consists of headquarters, three or four battalions, and the regimental depôt. Each battalion consists of headquarters, three companies, one mountain section of machine guns, and one nucleus of mobile militia. The *peace establishment* of the different units is as follows :—

—	Headquarters Regiment.	Headquarters Battalion.	Company.	M.G. Section.*	Nucleus of Mobile Militia.	Depôt.
Colonel	1	—	—	—	—	—
Lieutenant-Colonel or Majors	2	1	—	—	—	1
Captains	2–3	—	1	—	1	1
Lieutenants or 2nd Lieutenants	—	1	3	1	1	1
Medical Officers	1	1	—	—	—	—
Total	6–7	3	4	1	2	3 3 Attached Administrative Officers.
N.C.Os.	8	4	23	3	3	16
Other Ranks	4	6	127	11	27	18
Total	12	10	150	14	30	34

The total peace establishment of the "Alpini" is :—
570 Officers and
13,493 other ranks.
820 animals.

The "Alpini" are recruited locally, each battalion being allotted a recruiting zone and having its own mobilization

---
* *See* Chapter XI.

store. The peace garrisons are permanent. The men are carefully selected and form a "corps d'elite." On mobilization the battalions are reinforced by 38 companies of mobile militia. In addition there are 26 battalions (78 companies) of territorial militia.

The "Alpini" are kept well up to their peace establishment; indeed they usually exceed it during the summer months.

UNIFORM.

Grenadiers and Infantry of the Line.

Parade Dress.

Headdress :—(Grenadiers only), Officers—dark blue shako, with grenade and number of regiment.
  Men—dark blue shako or "berretto." white metal star with number of regiment, number of company (1 to 12) on red pompom.
Forage cap :—Officers—dark blue, red piping. Number of regiment on badge of crossed rifles (grenade for Grenadiers).
  Men—"Berretto" with number of regiment in white on a red star.
Greatcoat :—Officers—dark blue.
  Men—grey blue long-skirted, single-breasted with number of regiment in white on shoulder. If the greatcoat is worn on the march the skirts are usually buttoned back.
Tunic :—Officers—blue, double-breasted with turn-down black velvet collar : in full dress epaulettes are worn with a blue silk netted sash over the left shoulder. The sword belt is worn under the tunic. In undress, officers wear a single-breasted blue serge braided jacket.
  Men :—Single-breasted dark blue tunic with turned down collar showing brigade badge : white buttons, red piping, number of regiment in white on shoulder.
Cape :—Blue, with black velvet collar for officers.
Trousers :—Service dress pattern.
Ornaments and lace :—Silver.

Service Dress.

Forage cap :—Grey-green waterproof "berretto" with black peak.

Fatigue cap :—(For N.C.Os. and men only).

Tunic :—Officers—Grey-green Norfolk jacket with brigade badge on collar ; four outside pockets. Plain shoulder straps.

Men—Single-breasted grey-green loose tunic with flap concealing buttons ; two outside, one inside pocket. Brigade badge on collar.

Trousers :—Officers—Grey knickerbockers or breeches and putties.

Men—Grey-green trousers and putties.

Greatcoat :—Officers—long double-breasted grey-green greatcoat with rolled collar, two outside pockets.

Cloak :—Officers and men—long grey-green cloak with rolled collar.

In review order, parade dress is worn with epaulettes and shako.

In drill order, service dress is worn outside barracks ; inside barracks it is optional to wear either service or parade dress.

In marching order, service dress only is worn.

A service dress of grey drill was adopted in May, 1912, for use in hot weather. It is similar to the service dress of grey-green, but with red shoulder-straps for infantry.

Bersaglieri.

Parade Dress.

Headdress :—Black round stiff glazed felt hat with drooping green cock's feathers. Yellow metal ornament of a bugle, crossed carbines and a grenade with the number of the regiment.

Forage cap :—Turkish fez.

Cloak :—Long dark blue cape without ornaments.

Tunic :—Similar to line regiments, crimson edging, number of battalion on shoulder.

Trousers :—Dark blue, crimson stripe or piping.
Aiguillettes of green worsted cord with tassels.
Ornaments and stars—gold.
Cyclists wear the same uniform with leather gaiters and flannel shirts.

Service Dress.

Similar to that worn by line regiments except that the badges are made of red cloth. The hat has a grey-green covering.

"*Alpini.*"—Service dress only is worn.

Headdress :—A grey-green soft conical felt hat with the brim turned down in front, badge of crossed rifles and bugle with an eagle above, a raven's or peacock's feather at the side and the "Alpini" cockade.
Cloak :—Grey-green cloth with green collar.
Tunic :—Similar to service dress of line regiments with green facings.
Alpine boots reaching half-way to the knee, lacing up the front over the knickerbockers.
Trousers, knickerbockers ... } Of grey-green cloth.

Badges of Rank.

The badges of rank worn by officers consist of concentric rings round the forage cap, and stars worn on the shoulder strap, as follows :—

	On the head-dress.	On the shoulder strap.
Colonel	3 narrow rings. 1 broad ring.	3.
Lt.-Colonel	2 narrow rings. 1 broad ring.	2.
Major	1 narrow ring. 1 broad ring.	1.
Captain	3 rings.	3.
Lieutenant	2 rings.	2.
2nd Lieutenant	1 ring.	1.

Regimental commanders wear a white aigrette plume on ceremonial parades.

Field officers wear shoulder straps fringed with gold or silver lace.

Under officers are distinguished by stripes of gold or silver lace worn round the shako. Corporals wear red worsted stripes of a similar width.

"Marescialli"	Lace, interwoven with black silk.
Serjeant-Major	1 broad and 3 narrow stripes.
Serjeant	1 broad and 1 narrow stripe.
Corporal-Major	1 broad and 2 narrow stripes.
Corporal	1 broad and 1 narrow stripe.
Lance-Corporal	1 broad stripe.

Miscellaneous Badges.

A brigade major	Embroidered star on sleeve.
Adjutant	Lace stripe round the point of the collar.

Re-engaged under officers :—

12 years' service	3 lace stripes above the right elbow.
8 years' service	2 lace stripes above the right elbow.
4 years' service	1 lace stripe above the right elbow.
Marksmen (2 years)	Gold or silver rifle on sleeve.
„ (1 year)	Red worsted rifle on sleeve.
Cavalry or artillery scout	Star on the sleeve above the elbow.
First class troopers	Badge (horse's head) on sleeve.
Farriers, collar-makers, &c.	Distinctive badge on sleeve.

ARMAMENT AND EQUIPMENT.

Infantry of the Line.

Armament.—The infantry is armed with the Mannlicher rifle, model 1891.

Officers,* serjeant-majors, colour-serjeants and serjeant drummers carry a sword and revolver ; bandsmen carry a short sword ; stretcher-bearers a sword with a saw edge ; cyclists a carbine, 1891 model, with a hinged bayonet ; all other grades carry the 1891 rifle.

---

* Officers are gradually replacing revolvers by automatic pistols.

The principal data of the rifle, bayonet and ammunition are as follows:—

Weight without bayonet... ... 8 lb. 6 oz.
" with bayonet ... ... 9 " 2 "
Total length with bayonet ... 5 ft. 2½ inches.
" " without bayonet ... 4 " 2¾ "
Calibre ... ... 6·5 mm. (·256 inch).
Muzzle velocity ... ... 2395 f.s.
Number of grooves of rifling ... 4.

Greatest height of trajectory—
450 metres ... ... ·9 metre (2·95 feet).
1,000 " ... ... 9·25 metres (30·4 feet).
1,500 " ... ... 31·03 " (101·8 feet).
2,000 " ... ... 73·29 " (240·5 ").

The rifle is sighted from 330 to 2,200 yards, the extreme range being 3,300 yards. With the sight in the normal position the rifle is correctly sighted for 490 yards. The magazine holds six rounds and is loaded with a clip.

Bayonet, dagger-shaped—
Weight ... ... 12 oz.
Length ... ... 11¾ inches.
Scabbard ... ... Leather.

The charge of smokeless powder weighs 30·09 grains if of ballistite, 35·18 grains if of solenite. The bullet which is of lead with a casing of maillechort weighs 162·04 grains; the whole cartridge weighs 360 grains.

At a range of 100 yards the bullet will penetrate a steel plate ·23 inches thick or 43 inches of soft earth. At 500 yards it will penetrate 43 inches of rammed earth or 26 inches of loose sand.

For details of ammunition supply in war *see* Appendix IV.

Of the 168 rounds carried on the man, 96 are contained in four pouches (24 in each), 72 are carried in the lateral pockets of the knapsack.

Equipment.—Knapsack (containing 1 shirt, 1 pair of socks, 1 pair of slippers, 2 reserve rations and 72 cartridges), haversack, waterbottle, mess tin, belt, braces, one-fourth of a shelter tent, 1 entrenching tool.

The knapsack is of waterproof canvas (black for bersaglieri, brown for other infantry) and is fixed on the back by means of two braces of untanned leather. It can be rapidly taken off and put on again.

In addition to the above, "alpini" carry an alpenstock, 1 blanket and a pair of woollen gloves.

The total weight carried, including rifle and bayonet, is as follows:—

Infantry of the line ⎫
Grenadiers   ⎬ 56½ lbs.
Bersaglieri   ⎭
"Alpini" ... ... 64 lbs.

Bersaglieri Cyclists.—The bicycles are of the folding pattern, model 1904, invented by Captain Melli.

The following is the equipment carried:—

1 leather carrier, shaped to fasten to the interior of the bicycle frame, containing 2 days' reserve rations, 1 shirt and bicycle accessories.

1 carbine, model 1901, with hinged bayonet, fastened along the top of the frame, the butt to the front.

1 mess tin   ⎫
1 rolled cloak ⎬ Fastened below the saddle.

1 small entrenching tool carried below the saddle on the left side of the vertical portion of the frame.

The rest of the equipment is the same as that carried by the infantry, except that cyclists do not carry a knapsack. The 8 company telegraphists carry 2 cavalry micro-telephone apparatus and materials for tapping telegraph wires.

Rations. (*See* Appendix V.)

Regimental Transport.

Infantry of the Line and Bersaglieri.—Twenty-three 2-horsed wagons distributed as follows:—

Regimental headquarters: 2 wagons.

Each battalion: 7 wagons (four for rations and forage, one for baggage, one for ammunition, one medical wagon).

In addition to the above two 4-horsed canteen wagons are usually allowed per regiment, which carry "coffee bar" comforts for the troops. Water carts are usually hired for manœuvres, but do not form part of the regulation regimental transport.

The ammunition and medical wagons are the only vehicles allowed to go in the first line transport. The remaining wagons go in the second line, which is organized in two echelons.

Cyclist battalions have two motor cars and eleven motor cycles with battalion headquarters, and one motor car and two motor cycles with each company.

"*Alpini*" (Peace).

		Headquarters.		Per Company.
		Regimental.	Battalion.	
Pack mules	Baggage	3	3	4
	Rations (ordinary)	1	—	10
	" (reserve)	1	—	6
	Forage	2	—	—
	Explosives	—	1	—
	Ammunition	—	—	5
	Spare	—	3	1
	Total	7	7	26
Special mountain 2-horsed vehicles		—	2	1

In war the following increases are made :—

    Company ... ... 10 mules, 4 vehicles.
    Battalion headquarters ... 7 mules.
    Regimental ... ... 3 mules.

Entrenching Tools.

The following tools are carried by the infantry:—

Units.		Combined axe and pick.	Small spades.	Picks.	Combined axe and pick.	Saws.	Billhooks.	Shovels.	Various.
Infantry of the line and Bersaglieri	Company	26	80	2	2	1	3	4	11
	Battalion	104	320	8	8	6	12	16	44
	Regiment	312	960	24	32	20	36	48	106
Alpini	Company ...	13	33	60	5	8	3	6	20
	Battalion ...	39	99	180	32	12	20	24	80

In addition a few tools, useful when establishing a bivouac, are carried in the battalion transport.

Cyclists.—1 combined axe and pick or 1 small spade is carried per man. In addition 18 pioneers per company carry small engineer tools, and 16 cartridges of explosive gelatine, each 100 grammes, are carried in each company.

Disciplinary Companies and Military Penal Establishments.—The disciplinary companies and the military penal establishments constitute a special command, and consist of the following:—

Unit.	Station.	Colonel.	Majors.	Captains.	Lieutenants.	Doctors.	Account Officers.	N.C.Os. and men.	Total.
Command Staff	Gaeta	1	—	1	—	—	4	22	28
No. 1 Disciplinary Company	San Leo	—	—	2	6	—	—	42*	50
No. 2 Disciplinary Company	Francavilla-Fontana	—	—	2	6	—	—	42*	50
No. 3 Disciplinary Company	Gaeta (for San Leo)	—	—	2	6	—	—	34*	42
No. 4 Disciplinary Company	Fenestrelle	—	—	2	6	—	—	34*	42
Military Prison	Naples	—	1	1	4	1	1	33	41
Military Reformatory	Gaeta	—	1	2	5	1	2	56	67

* Cadres.

The disciplinary companies are of two characters :—

Nos. 1 and 2 for men of general bad character.

Nos. 3 and 4, special companies for men found guilty of theft.

The officers are taken from those who volunteer for this service, provided they are otherwise qualified. They wear the uniform of their regiment which they rejoin after a term of 6 or 7 years.

The non-commissioned officers and men are recruited either from the regular army or from men on unlimited leave who are 30 years old and have done 6 months' service with the colours.

The uniform, armament and equipment are as for the infantry of the line, except that the special companies wear a green pompom in the shako.

CHAPTER VIII.
CAVALRY.

Organization.—The Italian cavalry consist of 29 regiments, each regiment being composed of five squadrons and a depôt, each squadron is sub-divided into three troops. Sixteen of these regiments in addition have each a machine gun section.* Four of the regiments are heavy cavalry, eight are lancers and the remaining 17 are light cavalry. Each regiment bears a distinctive title as well as a number.

In peace time the regiments are organized in eight brigades of unequal strength ; brigades one to six form three cavalry divisions, each of two brigades of two regiments.

In time of war the organization of the cavalry divisions is the same, but a fourth† cavalry division is formed in addition : the remaining regiments not incorporated in the divisions form the protective cavalry.

(For peace distribution *see* Appendix VI.)

Commanders of Divisions and Staffs in Peace.

Cavalry Division.	Each Division.	3 Divisions.	—
1 Lieutenant or Major-General	1	3	⎫
Lieutenant-Colonel or Major	1	3	⎬ 2 Brigades in each Division.
Captain, Gen. Staff	1	3	⎭
Total	3	9	
Each Brigade	...	...	1 Major-General. 1 Staff Officer Captain.
			2
8 Brigades ...	...	...	16 officers.

* *See* Chap. XI. † *See* note on page 192.

Each regiment consists of headquarters, 5 squadrons and depôt ; 16 regiments also have a machine gun section.

Total peace establishment—
   1,060 Officers.
     58 Admin. & O.Cs. magazine.
  26,137 Other ranks.
  23,287 Horses.

Cavalry Regiment.
Peace Establishment.

Officers.	Headquarters.	Squad.	Depôt.	Total.	M.G. Section.	29 Regiments. 16 M.G. Sections.*
Colonel or Lieutenant-Colonel	1	—	—	1	—	29
Lieutenant-Colonel or Major extra	1–2†	—	1	2–3	—	66
Captain ...	1–2	5	1	7–8	—	211
Lieutenant or 2nd Lieutenant	1	15	4–5	20–21	1	609
Medical Officers ...	2	—	—	2	—	58
Administrative ...	—	—	1	1	—	29
Veterinary Officers	2	—	—	2	—	58
Total	8–10	20	7–8	35–38	1	1,060

* *See* Chap. XI.

† 8 Regiments have 2 Officers (Majors or Lieutenant-Colonels) extra at Headquarters.
   8 Regiments have 1 Captain extra at Headquarters.
    Attached Officers—
       Administrative ... ... 29 ⎫ Two for each
       Officers in charge of magazines ... 29 ⎭ regiment.

N.C.Os. and Men.	Headquarters.	5 Squadrons.	Depôt.	Total.	Machine Gun Section.	Total, 29 Regiments, 16 Machine Gun Sections.
N.C.Os.	13	140	13	—	3	—
Other Ranks	3	685	37	—	14	26,137
Total	16	825	50	—	17	—
Horses	17	750	—	767	23	23,287

Squadron—4 officers, 165 other ranks, 150 horses.
Depôt—7-8 officers, 50 other ranks.

—	Officers.	Other Ranks.	Horses.
Regiment, Headquarters	8-10	16	17
Summary of Depôt	7-8	50	—
Machine Gun Section, if part of Regiment	1	17	23
Five Squadrons	20	825	750
Total	36-39	908	790

War Establishment.

Unit.	Officers.	Rank and File.	Horses.
Squadron	4	149	139
Regiment	31	784	714

The actual strength of a squadron is below the peace establishment and averages about 132.

NOTE.—*Cavalry*, increase of, in 1912.

The following increase to the Cavalry has been made in 1912 :—

15th Lodi Regiment ... ... 1 Squadron.
16th Lucca Regiment... ... ... 2 Squadrons.
18th Piacenza Regiment ... ... 1 Squadron.
19th Guide Regiment... ... ... 1 Squadron.

These units are probably to form the nucleus of a Cavalry Regiment in Libya.

The increase to the cavalry will be :—

1 major.
5 captains.
15 lieutenants or 2nd lieutenants.

and probably
825 other ranks and 750 horses.

These numbers are not included in the totals already given.

Specially trained N.C.Os. and Men.

Selected scouts are N.C.Os. and men specially trained in reconnaissance duty. All N.C.Os. may qualify ; the number of private soldiers is limited to 5 per squadron. The appointment lasts for 1 year, after which men may re-qualify. They wear a special badge, and are mounted on picked horses ; the privates receive $\frac{1}{2}d.$ a day extra pay.

1st class horsemen are men chosen annually for their special aptitude in riding and training horses. They wear a special badge.

Pigeon Post.—One N.C.O. per squadron has to pass a fifteen day course in the management of carrier pigeons. Four pigeon baskets are allotted to each squadron.

Telegraphists.—Selected officers, N.C.Os. and men are sent periodically to go through a four-month course in telegraphy under engineer officers.

Uniform.

Parade Dress.

Headdress.—The heavy cavalry (regiments one to four) wear a helmet of white metal with a gilt crest, no plume. The remainder wear a colback or busby of black sealskin with a red pompom; in full dress an upright eagle's feather is worn in the busby.

Forage cap, as for infantry.

Greatcoat.—Grey cloth, double breasted, with fixed cape.

Tunic.—Dark blue cloth, single breasted, turn down collar; piping, facings and collar patch vary according to the regiment.

Trousers.—Service dress pattern.

Boots.— Long boots are worn by officers only. Rank and file wear black leather gaiters, ankle boots and spurs.

Distinctive Badges.—Heavy cavalry: white grenade with number of regiment. Lancers: number of regiment placed on two crossed lances and surmounted by a crown. Light cavalry: a "cor de chasse," enclosing the number of the regiment, and surmounted by a crown. Officers detached from a regiment wear a white star on black ground surmounted by a crown. These badges are worn on the headdress or forage cap. The number of the squadron is shown in white numerals on the busby pompom.

Service Dress.

Forage Cap.—Of grey-green waterproof cloth, black leather peak.

Fatigue Cap.

Tunic.—Grey-green Norfolk jacket with rolled collar and four outside pockets. The collar and shoulder straps are of the distinctive colour of the regiment.

Cloak of grey-green cloth, reaching to the knees and buttoning round the throat.

Trousers of grey-green cloth, tight at the knee and worn with gaiters and ankle boots.

Service dress is being gradually issued to troops as the old pattern uniform wears out; the issue should have been completed towards the end of 1912.

A service dress of grey cotton drill was adopted in May, 1912, for use in hot weather.

It is similar in appearance to the grey-green service dress.

Armament (for machine guns see *Chap. XI).*—Officers, under officers, trumpeters, and pioneers carry a sword and revolver; other ranks are armed with sword and carbine. The lancer and heavy cavalry regiments carry the lance.

The carbine is of the 1891 pattern with a hinged bayonet; it is carried in a bucket on the off-side of the saddle. The construction and calibre of the carbine are similar to that of the rifle, except for the fact that the bolt is turned down.

The carbine is 35·43 inches long (49·8 inches with the bayonet fixed) and weighs 6·9 lbs.; it is sighted from 330 to 1,640 yards, and has an extreme range of 3,000 yards.

The revolver.—Pattern 1889, 6 cartridges, calibre ·407 inches, weight 2 lbs., length 9·25 inches. Pattern 1874 same calibre as 1889 pattern; weight $2\frac{1}{2}$ lbs., length 11·41 inches. The cartridge weighs 262·34 grains, the bullet 175 grains, the powder charge 9·25 grains.

The lance is of hollow steel with a blue pennon. Length, 10 ft. 4 in.; weight, 4·73 lbs.

The sword.—1900 pattern; slightly curved; ordinary guard. Total length, including hilt, 3 ft. 5 in.; length of blade, 2 ft. 11 in.; weight, 2 lbs. 4 ozs.; steel scabbard, weight 1 lb. 8 ozs.

Ammunition.—On mobilization, 96 rounds are carried on the man for the carbine, 18 for the revolver. Twenty-four rounds of carbine ammunition are carried in a leather bandolier, and 36 rounds in each saddle-bag (36 of the latter are arranged in pouches which can be attached to the bandolier if required).

For *ammunition supply, see* Appendix IV.

Equipment.

The Man.—Belt, mess tin, bandolier, sword, carbine.

The Horse.—Bridle, bit, and bridoon; head collar (English pattern); saddle on folded blanket. Australian girths, leather surcingle; two sheepskin saddlebags (containing 72 rounds of ammunition, two days' reserve rations, one pair of socks, cleaning kit, fatigue cap); cornsack, greatcoat carried over pommel.

Average weight carried by man, 7 to 11 lbs.
„   „   „   horse (heavy cavalry and lancers) 18 st. 9 lbs.
„   „   „   „   (light cavalry), 18 st. 1 lb.

Regimental Transport (Peace and War).

	Regtl. Staff.	Squadron.	Total per Regt.	
			Wagons.	Horses.
Wagons (3 horses)	3	1	8	24
Wagons (forage and general service)	—	1	5	15
Canteen wagon (2 horses)	1	—	1	2
	4	2	14	41

Rations (see *Appendix V*).

Tools and Explosives.—The tools carried by the cavalry pioneers are lighter than those used by the infantry, and include a number of special tools for the interruption and repair of telegraph lines.

Distribution.

Unit.	Shovels, Picks, &c.	Axes, Saws, &c.	Cartridges of Explosive Gelatine.
Squadron—			
Including transport	18	20	28
Excluding transport	6	10	4
Regiment—			
Including transport	110	120	140
Excluding transport	30	50	20

The figures are approximate.

CHAPTER IX.

ARTILLERY.

Composition.*

The artillery is composed of the following units :—

One regiment of horse artillery.
Thirty-six regiments of field artillery.
Two regiments of mountain artillery.
Two regiments of heavy field artillery.
Ten regiments of fortress artillery.

Horse Artillery.

Organization.—There is one regiment of horse artillery composed of the regimental staff, four groups of two batteries each, four transport companies, and a depôt. The regimental headquarters are at Milan.

The regiment is commanded by a colonel or lieutenant-colonel. Each group of batteries and the depôt is commanded by a major or lieutenant-colonel. A lieutenant-colonel or major commands the four transport companies. Batteries and transport companies are commanded by captains. On mobilization the regiment provides one group of 2 batteries for each cavalry division.

The regimental staff includes four veterinary officers and two medical officers.

In 1910 the batteries, which had formerly been of 6 guns, adopted the 4-gun organization. Each battery is now composed of four guns, seven ammunition wagons, one forge wagon, one battery wagon, one forage wagon; one spare gun carriage, three spare wheels and 11 spare poles are distributed among the various vehicles. Each gun is drawn by six horses.

---

*See note on page 85.

Peace Establishment.

Unit.	Officers.	Administrative Officers.	N.C.Os.	Men.	Horses.	Remarks.
Headquarters	20	2	27	2	15	*Including 1 sub-officer, instructor in equitation.
1 Battery	4	—	27	93	108	
1 Transport Co.	3	—	23	67	40	
Depôt	4	2	22	36	—	
Total for regiment	68	4	1,407*	1,068†		†Including officers' chargers.

War Establishment.

—	Officers.	Rank and File.	Total Personnel.	Horses.
Regimental Staff	20	27	44	11
1 Battery	4	155	159	183
Total Regt. (8 Batteries)	49	1,267	1,316	1,475

Field Artillery.

Organization.—There are at present 30 regiments of Field Artillery. Six more regiments are being formed and when the artillery re-organization is completed there will be 36 regiments. Each regiment consists of :—

    Headquarters.
    2 groups of batteries
    1 transport company.
    1 depôt.

Batteries armed with the 75A gun have 6 guns, and those armed with the 1906 Krupp gun have 4 or 6 guns.

Twenty-four regiments have five batteries, and each of these has a depôt battery.

Groups in these regiments are two or three batteries.

Some groups are formed of mountain guns, each group consisting of three batteries.

The remaining regiments have also groups of three batteries each.

The 24 regiments with depôt batteries form bases of formation for the batteries of the mobile militia.

The Regiment.—A colonel or lieutenant-colonel commands the regiment.

Groups and depôts are commanded by lieutenant-colonels or majors.

Batteries and transport companies are commanded by captains.

The staff of a regiment includes two medical and two veterinary officers.

The first twelve regiments, each of six batteries divided into two groups, form the corps artillery of the twelve army corps, the remaining 24 regiments constituting the divisional artillery of 24 out of the 25 divisions. Regiments of divisional artillery are formed of two groups—one of three and one of two batteries.

For details of the transport companies *see* Chap. XIV.

The 36 depôts each contain regular cadres for one mobile militia battery; the depôts when reinforced by men of the mobile militia are expected to furnish 63 batteries in case of mobilization.

Peace Establishment.

Units.	Officers.	Administrative Officers.	Sub-Officers and N.C.Os.	Soldiers.	Horses.	Remarks.
Headquarters	11	1	19	—	—	* These batteries are separate from the Mountain Artillery Regiments. † Including 22 sub-officers, Instructors in Equitation ‡ Including officers' chargers.
1 Battery	3 to 4	—	26	74	60	
1 Mountain Battery*	3 to 4	—	44	106	70	
1 Transport Co.	3	—	23	67	40	
1 Depôt with Battery	5	1	46	51	47	
Depôt	5	1	20	17	7	
Total for 36 Regiments	1,361	108	26,190†		15,900‡	

War Establishment.

Field Battery.

1 battery, 4 officers, 152 other ranks, 122 horses.

Mountain Artillery.

Organization.—There are 2 regiments of mountain artillery with headquarters at Turin and Vicenza respectively.

Each regiment is composed of 4 groups of 3 batteries each and a depôt. Each regiment is commanded by a colonel or lieutenant-colonel.

The groups of batteries and the depôt are commanded by majors or lieutenant-colonels.

Batteries are commanded by captains.

There are 2 or 3 medical officers and 4 veterinary officers with each regiment.

The batteries are organized in 3 echelons, namely, the

fighting echelon and the battery ammunition column, both of which have pack transport, and the battery park, which has wheeled transport. 70 mm. Batteries have 6 guns, and 65 mm. Batteries 4. In the former, gun, carriage, wheels, and 2 boxes ammunition are carried by 5 mules, and the latter have 1 extra mule for the shield. Mules carry from 224 lbs. to 317 lbs.

On mobilization, the mountain artillery act in conjunction with the "alpini" as "troupes de couverture," and do not form part of the army corps organization. The depôts organize 15 additional batteries from the mobile militia.

Peace Establishment.

Unit.	Officers.	Administrative Officers.	Sub-officers and N.C.Os.	Soldiers.	Horses and Mules.	Remarks.
Headquarters	21–22	1	23–24*	2	5	*Includes Trumpeters, Pioneers, Saddlers, &c.
1 Battery	4	—	44*	106	70	
1 Depôt	5	5	22*	49	24	
Total, 2 Regiments	149	12	3,790		1,870†	†Includes chargers for officers.

War Establishment.

Unit.	Officers.	Rank and File.	Total Personnel.	* Horses and Mules.
1 Battery	5	185	190	85
Ammunition column and park	2	148	150	88

* Including Officers' Horses.

Heavy Field Artillery.

Organization.—There are two regiments of heavy field artillery, each regiment being composed of headquarters, four groups of batteries of two or three batteries each, ten batteries in all, and a depôt.

A colonel or lieutenant-colonel commands the regiment. Lieutenant-colonels or majors command groups and the depôt, Batteries are commanded by captains, and have 4 guns.

Two medical and two veterinary officers belong to each regiment.

Peace Establishments.

Unit.	Officers.	Administrative Officers.	Sub-officers, N.C.Os., Trumpeters, Artificers, &c.	Soldiers.	Horses.	Remarks.
Headquarters...	15	1	27	—	15	
A Battery ...	4	—	26	74	16	
Depôt	4	3	20	17	7	
Total, 2 Regiments	118	8	2,128	1,312*		*Including officers' chargers.

War Establishment.

1 battery.
4 officers, 137 to 172 other ranks, 4 guns.
Each gun or ammunition wagon is drawn by 6 horses.

Fortress Artillery.

Organization.—In 1910, the coast defence and fortress artillery which had previously been separate organizations were amalgamated under the name of fortress artillery.

Under this arrangement the fortress artillery is grouped into ten regiments composed of 18 groups of fortress companies and 15 groups of coast defence companies, and comprising 55 fortress and 43 coast defence companies and 10 depôts.

Each regiment is composed of a regimental staff, three or more groups of companies, and a depôt. Each regiment is commanded by a colonel or lieutenant-colonel, each group and the depôt by a lieutenant-colonel or major.

Companies are commanded by captains.

Each regiment has two or three medical officers.
The details of this organization are shown in Appendix VII.
The five companies of artillery artificers are merged into
the new organization.

On mobilization the active army garrisons the various
fortresses and mobilizes the siege park. The depôts
mobilize 78 companies of mobile militia, while a further
reinforcement of 100 companies of territorial militia will
eventually become available.

Fortress artillery companies are armed with 5·87-in. guns
and howitzers, 8·2-in. mortars, and 4·7-in. guns of various
patterns.

Peace Establishment.

Unit.	Officers.	Administrative Officers.	Sub-officers, N.C.Os., Artificers, &c.	Soldiers.	Horses.	Remarks.
Headquarters ...	10–14	—	18 to 30	5–7	3–5	10 regiments.
1 Company ...	3–4	—	20	90	—	33 groups.
1 Depôt ...	4–5	3	19	20	—	98 companies.
Total 10 Regts.	493	30	11,736		60	10 depôts.

War Establishment.

Unit.	Officers.	Rank and File.	Total Personnel.
1 Fortress Company	3	130–200	133–203
1 Coast Defence Company ...	7	240	247

NOTE.—By orders, dated December 9th, 1911, the following new units have been added, probably to form part of a new colonial army in Libya :—

Field Artillery (1 Battery each Regiment)—
5th, 11th, 16th, 17th, 21st, and 27th Regiments ... } 6 Batteries.

Mountain Artillery—
  1st Regiment ... ... 2 Batteries.
  2nd   ,, ... 3 ,,
  22nd Field Artillery Regt. 1 ,,
Fortress Artillery—
  3rd Regiment ... ... 2 Companies.
  6th ,, ... 2 ,,
  7th ,, ... 2 ,,
  10th ,, ... 2 ,,

The probable increase of numbers due to this is:—

	Officers.	Other ranks.	Horses.	Guns.
Field Artillery— Two groups: 2 Lieut.-Cols. or Majors 6 Captains 12 Lieutenants		600	360	24
Mountain Artillery— Four groups: 4 Lieut.-Cols. or Majors 12 Captains 36 Lieutenants		1,800	840	72
Fortress Artillery— 4 groups (each of 3 Cos.) 4 Lieut.-Cols. or Majors 12 Captains 36 Lieutenants		1,320	—	—

(8 companies were formed by July, 1912.)

Technical Service of Artillery.

In 1910 the technical service of artillery was separated from the combatant service.

The personnel of the technical service is as follows:—
  1 Lieutenant or Major-General, Inspector of Artillery Construction.
  1 General Officer.
  6 Major-Generals or Colonels, principal directors.
  10 Field Officers, sub-directors.
  60 other officers.

Officers desirous of entering the technical service must attend specified courses for 2 years at civilian or military establishments. After this they must successfully go through a superior technical artillery course.

The limits for retirement for age are about 4 years higher than in the combatant branch.

Uniform.

Parade Dress.

Headdress (Horse Artillery only).—Black shako with yellow metal ornament with regimental badge ; a long horsehair plume fixed in a red pompom is worn in full dress.

The regimental badges are as follows :—

Horse Artillery : 2 crossed swords above 2 crossed guns.
Field Artillery : 2 crossed guns, surmounted by a grenade.
Fortress Artillery : 2 crossed guns and 2 rifles below a grenade.
Technical Artillery : similar to field artillery with a cross of Savoy on the grenade.
Mountain Artillery : 2 crossed guns and a bugle below the regimental number.

Greatcoat.—Double-breasted, of grey cloth with long fixed cape.

Tunic.—Similar to cavalry, dark blue gorget (black velvet for officers) with yellow stripes ; dark blue cuffs.

Trousers.—Service dress pattern.

Ornaments.—Gold.

Service Dress.

The mountain artillery wear a uniform similar to the "alpini" ; the remainder of the artillery have a service dress similar to the cavalry.

A service dress of grey drill was adopted in May, 1912. It is similar to the grey-green service dress, but has yellow shoulder straps for artillery.

Special Artillery Badges.

1st class "layer" : gun in yellow cloth on left sleeve.
Scout : 5-pointed yellow star embroidered on sleeve.
Range-finder : 8-pointed gold star embroidered on black cloth, left arm.
Assistant range-finder : same badge in yellow worsted.

Armament and Equipment.

The horse and field artillery are both armed with the 75 mm. Q.F. Krupp gun, model 1906. The Italian Government have had considerable difficulty as regards the re-armament of their artillery owing to their adoption in 1901 of a 75 mm. Krupp gun with rigid mounting which proved to be by no means up to modern requirements. The 1906 pattern has proved more satisfactory, and the issue of the new gun was to have been completed by the end of 1911. In November, 1911, there were still 93 field batteries armed with the 1901 model 75A gun. In May, 1910, it had been decided to replace these by a new model. After a long delay a Deport gun manufactured in Italy was adopted, and the batteries of this gun should be delivered by July, 1913. In this way there will be two models of guns in use in the Italian regular army, both, however, using the same ammunition. The materials for the guns are sent to Italy in the rough and are finished in the Italian arsenals. The ammunition is made in Italy.

The mountain artillery 70 mm. gun is an accelerated firer, but is not an up-to-date weapon. Experiments have been carried out with a 65 mm. Q.F. mountain gun of Italian construction, with which the mountain artillery will gradually be re-armed ; 32 batteries will be armed with this gun in April, 1913.

The 149 mm. field howitzer for heavy field artillery was adopted in 1910, in preference to a lighter weapon with a calibre of 105 mm.

The following table gives some details of these guns :—

Data.	Krupp, 75 mm. Mod. 1906.	Krupp, 75 mm. Mod. 1906, Horse Art.	Deport, 75 mm. Mod. 1911.	Mountain Art., 70 mm.	Mountain Art., 65 mm.	Howitzer, 149 mm.
Gun.						
Weight with breech mechanism	760·5 lbs.	760·5 lbs.	640 lbs.	220·5 lb.	220·5 lbs.	1,918 lbs.
Calibre	2·95″	2·95″	2·95″	2·76″	2·76″	5·87″
Total length	88·5″	88·5″	83·94″	45·27″	46·06″	82·28″
Gun Carriage.						
Weight with gun	2,204½ lbs.	2,164 lbs.	2,293 lbs.	854 lbs.	1,256 lbs.	3,119 lbs. (without gun)
Length of trail	103″	113·8″	106·1″	—	88·2″	151·6″
Max. elevation	16°	16°	50°	21°	20°	43°
Max. depression	10°	10°	15° 30′	12°	8°	5°
Length of recoil on gun carriage	51″	51″ to 55″	39·37″	—	33·6″	49·2″

Data.	Krupp, 75 mm. Mod. 1906.	Krupp, 75 mm. Mod. 1906, Horse Art.	Deport, 75 mm. Mod. 1911.	Mountain Art., 70 mm.	Mountain Art., 65 mm.	Howitzer, 149 mm.
Gun Carriage—ctd.						
Gun limber, weight loaded	1,508 lbs.	1,382 lbs.	—	—	—	1,047 lbs.
Wagon limber, weight loaded	1,497 lbs.	1,382 lbs.	—	—	—	2,941 lbs.
Wagon body, weight loaded	2,354½ lbs.	2,220 lbs.	—	—	—	3,968 lbs.
Shields, thickness	·157″	·157″	·157″	None	·157″	·157″
Sights	telescopic panoramic	telescopic panoramic	telescopic panoramic	not telescopic	telescopic panoramic	telescopic panoramic
Telephones	yes	—	yes	—		
Shrapnel, weight of, with fuze	14·3 lbs.	14·3 lbs.	14·3 lbs.	10·8 lbs.	9·3 lbs.	88·2 lbs.
Fuzes, extreme range	6,452 yds.	6,452 yds.	6,452 yds.	5,468 yds.	5,575 yds.	7,327 yds.
Muzzle velocity, feet per second	1,673 ft.	1,673 ft.	1,673 ft.	1,148 ft.	1,132 ft.	541 to 984 ft.
Weights, gun and limber	3,712 lbs.	3,547 lbs.	—	—	—	6,393 lbs.
Wagon and limber	3,850 lbs.	3,57¼ lbs.	—	—	—	6,459 lbs.

Armament (*Personnel*).

—	Officers.	N.C.Os.	Gunners and Drivers.	Escort to Train.	*Other men.
Field Artillery	Sword and revolver†	Sword and revolver	Short sword	Carbine, 1891 pattern, bayonet	Sword
Horse Artillery	Sword and revolver†	Sword and revolver	Sword-bayonet, revolver	—	Sword
Mountain Artillery	Sword and revolver†	Revolver, short sword	Carbine, sword-bayonet	—	—
Fortress Artillery	Sword and revolver†	Sword and revolver	Rifle, 1891 pattern, sword-bayonet	—	—

* Shoeing smiths are armed with revolver only.
† Or automatic pistol.

Equipment.

Field Artillery.—On the man. Haversack, canteen, belt, cartridge pouch, cross-belt.

On the horse. Saddle, bridle and head collar, feed bag and cloak rolled in front of saddle, two saddlebags, wallet and quarter of shelter tent behind saddle.

Horse Artillery.—On the man. The same as field artillery without cross belt, pouch, or rear wallet on saddle.

Mountain Artillery.—Equipment similar to "alpini."

Fortress Artillery.—Equipment similar to infantry, with only one ammunition pouch.

Ammunition per Gun (War). 1st Line Organizations.	75 Mod. 1906.	75 Horse Artillery.	Mountain.		149 mm. Howitzer.
			70 A	65 mm.	
With the Battery	320	284	350*	575	64 per gun
Corps or Divisional Column	117	—	110	†	64 ,,
Corps Artillery Park	96	—	—	—	72 ,,
Cavalry Division Park	—	85	—	—	—
Total	533	369	460	575	200

* Includes rounds carried in battery column and park.
† Not known.

Both shrapnel and H.E. shell are carried, the latter filled with "pertite" which is practically picric acid.

In Field Artillery 32 rounds are carried in the gun and wagon limber, 64 in the ammunition body.

Horse Artillery batteries have 24 rounds in the gun limber, 24 in the wagon limber, and 56 in the wagon body.

Heavy batteries have 12 rounds in the wagon limber, and 20 in the wagon body.

Shells are carried ready fuzed. Percussion detonators to insert when loaded are carried separately. The fuze is made of metal, has a time and percussion double-action and burns for 20 seconds.

The fuzes are set by a metal fuze-setter, which is set to the required graduation. It is then dropped over the fuze and one twist sets it mechanically.

Small Arm Ammunition.
36 rounds per rifle or carbine (on the man).
18 ,, ,, revolver (on the man).

Regimental Transport.

Wheeled Transport (Excluding guns).	F. Art. 75 A.	F. Art., Mod. 1906.	Horse Art., Mod. 1906.	149 m.m. Howitzers.	70 m.m. Mountain Gun	65 m.m. Mountain Gun.
Ammunition wagons...	7	12* or 18	13	8†	—	—
,, carts......	—	—	—	—	5	7
Other wagons	3	3* or 4	5	—	—	—
,, carts	—	—	—	—	4	1

* For 4-gun battery.
† Transport details not known.

Mountain Artillery.—Mountain artillery batteries have 76 pack mules with the fighting echelon, and 64 pack mules in the battery ammunition column.

Entrenching Tools—
 Field batteries carry—
  57 picks.
  60 shovels.
 Mountain batteries carry—
  40 light picks.
  46 short shovels.

These are carried by a special pioneer section.
In addition a small number of cutting and other tools are carried.

General Remarks.—The process of increasing the number of field artillery regiments from 30 to 36 and the creation of two new regiments of heavy field artillery is likely to prove both long and difficult.

It is the opinion of good judges that proper value will not be obtained from the new re-organization until the summer of 1913.

CHAPTER X.

PART I.

ENGINEERS.*

The Engineers of the Italian Army consist of six regiments and one battalion of "Specialisti." These units are subdivided as follows in peace :—

1st and 2nd regiments " Zappatori " (Sappers).

Each regiment consists of :—
Headquarters.
4 battalions, each of 3 field companies.
† 1 battalion of 2 companies.
1 depôt.

3rd regiment—" Telegraphisti " (Telegraph).

The regiment consists of headquarters, 5 telegraph battalions, each of 3 companies, a† separate telegraph company, 2 transport companies and a depôt.

4th regiment—" Pontieri " (Bridging).

The regiment consists of headquarters, 3 pontoon battalions —in all 8 companies, 1 lagoon battalion of 2 companies, 3 transport companies, and a depôt.

5th regiment—" Minatori " (Miners).

The regiment consists of headquarters, 4 battalions, each of 3 companies, a separate company*, 1 transport company, 1 depôt.

6th regiment—." Ferrovieri " (Railway).

Headquarters.
2 railway battalions, each of 3 companies.
1 section for working the railway line.
1 automobile battalion of 2 companies.
1 depôt.

---

* For peace distribution *see* Appendix VIII.
† These units have been formed in 1912 by Royal Decrees dated 7th December, 1911, and 27th June, 1912, and will probably form part of the new Colonial Army.

The "Specialisti" battalion.

Headquarters.
4 mobile companies.
1 company of mechanics.
1 wireless section.
1 photographic section.
1 transport company.

The duties of this battalion include details in connection with balloon parks and dirigibles, electric searchlights, wireless telegraphy, telephones and telephotography.

The peace establishments are shown in the following table, headquarters and staffs of battalions being included in regimental headquarters.

Each regiment is commanded by a colonel, or lieutenant-colonel, and each depôt and battalion by a lieutenant-colonel or major.

Officers attached for administrative purposes, and officers in charge of stores, are shown under the heading "Administrative Officers."

Each regiment has (usually) two medical officers.

Each company has a captain and two or three other officers.

Peace Establishments.
ENGINEERS.

Units.	Officers.	Administrative Officers.	N.C.Os.	Privates.	Horses.	Remarks.
1st and 2nd Regts.—						* Includes 3 officers' chargers.
Headquarters	15	—	25 or 26	3	—	1 regt. has
1 Field Company	3	—	14	86	—	2 Cos., 1
1 Transport Company	3	—	20	70	43*	regt. has
Depôt	5	4 or 5	13	28	—	1 Co.
Total for 2 Regts.	130	9	3,218		86	
3rd Regt.—						* Includes 3 officers' chargers.
Headquarters	18	—	62	3	—	
1 Company	3	—	18	112	—	
1 Transport Company	6	—	23	46	40	
Depôt	6	4	21	53	—	
Total for Regt.	82	4	2,400		83*	

Units.	Officers.	Administrative Officers.	N.C.Os.	Privates.	Horses.	Remarks.
4th Regt.—						*Including 9 officers' chargers.
Headquarters	16	—	27	3	—	
1 Company	3	—	16	94	—	
1 Lagoon Company	3	—	26 or 27	103	—	
Transport Company	3	—	23	67	40	
Depôt	5	4	14	27	—	
Total for Regt.	62	4	1,480		129*	
5th Regt.—						*Including 3 officers' chargers.
Headquarters	17	—	23	3	—	
1 Company	3	—	11	89	6*	
1 Transport Company	3	—	23	67	40	
Depôt	5	4	15	27	—	
Total for Regt.	64	4	1,458		115*	
6th Regt.—						
Headquarters	13	2	24	2	12	
1 Railway Company	4	—	22 or 23	149 or 150	—	
1 Section	6	—	68	60	—	
1 Automobile Company	4	—	25	125	—	
Depôt	5	4	1,220			
Total for Regt.	56	6	1,385		12	
"Specialisti" Battalion:—						
Headquarters	16	10	—	—	—	
1 Mobile Company	4	—	19	101	—	*Including 3 officers' chargers.
1 Company Mechanics	3	—	21	129	—	
1 Wireless Section	4	—	24	80	—	
1 Photo Section	2	1	11	21	—	
1 Transport Company	3	—	34	66	80	
Total for Regt.	44	11	900		83*	

War Organization and Establishment.

The engineer regiments furnish the following units on mobilization :—

1st and 2nd Regiments.
  (1) 1 field company to each division.
  (2) 1 bridging section to each division.
  (3) 1 engineer park to each army corps.
  (4) 1 engineer park to each field army.
  (5) Details that may be required in fortresses and in siege operations.

The following is the approximate war establishment of the above units :—

	Men.		Horses.		Vehicles.	
	Officers.	R. & F.	Saddle.	Draught.	2-wheeled.	4-wheeled.
Field Company	5	265	3	20	1	4
Pontoon Section	1	30	3	32	—	7
Army Corps park	3	64	10	58	1	12
Army park	5	106	15	104	2	21

The personnel of the transport is composed of men from the engineer transport companies.

3rd Regiment.
  1 telegraph park to the headquarters of the supreme commander.
  1 telegraph park to each army.
  1 telegraph park to each army corps.
Approximate war establishment of a telegraph park :—
  4 officers.
  116 non-commissioned officers and men.
  59 horses.
  14 vehicles.

A telegraph park carries material for the construction of 40 miles of telegraph line.

4th Regiment.—To each army in the field this regiment supplies one pontoon brigade consisting of two bridging trains, each composed of one pontoon company and transport. The war establishment of these units is as follows :—

Pontoon Brigade.	Men.		Horses.		Vehicles.
	Officers.	R. & F.	Saddle.	Draught.	4-wheeled.
Brigade Staff...	4	9	7	—	—
1 Pontoon Company	5	240	5	—	—
Transport Company	3	153	14	196	46
Total of Brigade	20	795	45	392	92

For details of bridging material *see* page 98.

The lagoon companies are intended for service at Venice; their general organization is similar to that of the pontoon companies, but they have a special material for service on the lagoons; their war establishment amounts to 280 men per company.

5th Regiment.—This regiment supplies one brigade (of two or three companies) to each field army. Companies are of the same strength as in the 1st and 2nd regiments.

6th Regiment.—The railway battalions besides bringing their companies to war strength provide two labour parks and one executive park.

The war establishment of a railway company is :—
    5 officers.
    265 rank and file.
    22 horses.
    5 vehicles.

Transport Companies.—The transport companies are distributed on mobilization throughout the corps of engineers to provide personnel for the transport.

Mobile Militia Engineer Companies.—On mobilization, the mobile militia furnish the following units :—

Field companies	24
Telegraph companies	6
"Specialisti" companies	1
Pontoon companies	4
Lagoon companies	1
Sapper and miner companies	12
Railway companies	6
Transport companies	4
Total	58

Territorial Militia.—The territorial militia mobilize 30 engineer companies.

Uniform.—Parade dress.

Forage cap, as worn by infantry, with red piping and badges.

Trousers, Service dress pattern.

Tunic and greatcoat, as worn by infantry, with distinctive badges ; tunic, collar and cuffs black with red lines.

Ornaments—gold.

In addition, the following special dress is worn :—

Railway companies, when on locomotive duty, tunic and trousers of black fustian, goatskin cap, brown cloth greatcoat.

Automobilist companies :—
    Goatskin cap, motor goggles, blue blouse, waterproof cloak, black woollen gloves.

Lagoon companies :—
    Blue tam-o-shanter or straw hat, blue flannel shirt with badges of rank on sleeve, linen trousers.

Service Dress.

Similar to that worn by the infantry, with distinctive badge on tunic collar.

The grey drill service dress recently introduced has crimson shoulder straps.

Badges of Rank.

Similar to those worn by infantry.

Miscellaneous Badges.

Automobilists	Yellow metal automobile on the cap and on the left sleeve.
Railway regiment	Winged wheel with lightning flashes and two crossed axes under a grenade.
Lagoon mechanician	Screw with three blades in red wool on the left sleeve.
Telegraph transmitter	Sheaf of arrows, in red wool on the left sleeve.
First class waterman	Crimson anchor on left sleeve.

Armament and Equipment.

Under officer	Infantry sword and revolver.
Corporals and private soldiers	Carbine, 1891 pattern, and bayonet. The men of the train companies who are not employed on escort duty carry a sword only.

The equipment is similar to that carried by the infantry, except that only one ammunition pouch is worn, and in the field companies each man carries an entrenching tool.

Bridging Material.

Divisional Bridging Section.—
4 four-horsed wagons carrying in all two pontoons, baulks and transoms.
1 ,, ,, ,, baulks and transoms.
1 ,, ,, ,, four trestles.
1 ,, ,, ,, baggage, rations, &c.

With pontoons only the section can construct a bridge 22 yards long ; with pontoons and trestles a bridge 44 yards long can be built.

The pontoons can be used as boats, with a carrying capacity of 24 armed infantry besides the crew ; they can also be made into rafts to carry 52 armed infantry or guns and limbers, or six horses and men.

Bridging Train.

The material carried by a bridging train is sufficient to throw the following lengths of bridge :—

(1) Pontoon only... ... ... 200 yards.
(2) Trestles only... ... ... 70 ,,
(3) Double pontoon ... ... 80 ,,
(4) Trestles and pontoons ... ... 250 ,,

The pontoon can be used as boats or rafts, and have approximately the same carrying capacity as those carried by the divisional section. A raft can also be made of two double pontoons, capable of carrying any of the following loads :—162 men, 12 field guns or wagons, 20 horses.

Transport.

(1) *A Field Company—*
4 light four-horsed engineer wagons.
1 two-horsed company wagon.
The engineer wagons contain entrenching tools, explosive gelatine, some survey instruments and camping material.
Weight—empty ... ... 1,500 lbs.
    loaded ... ... 2,343 ,,

The company wagon carries baggage, rations and a small quantity of material.
Weight—empty ... ... 970 lbs.

(2) *A Telegraph Park.*
The transport is organized in three sections :—
(a) Electric telegraph section.

             Weight in lbs.
             Loaded.
3 four-horsed light wagons 4,300
3 ,, heavy ,, ... 5,180

(b) Optical signalling section.

	Weight in lbs. Loaded.
4 two-horsed vehicles	860

(c) Reserve section.

2 four-horsed wagons	3,530
2 two-horsed „	1,100

(3) *A Bridging Train.* (All four-horsed wagons.)
    27 pontoon wagons. Average 5,000 lbs.
    10 wagons, carrying chesses and transoms.
    3 trestle wagons.
    3 miscellaneous wagons.
    3 baggage and ration wagons.

Entrenching Tools.

The following entrenching tools are carried by a field company (including divisional bridging section) :—

—	Saws.	Picks.	Shovels.	Billhooks.	100 Gram Gelatine Cartridges.	Primers.
War ...	10	89	137	24	1584	576

in addition to other miscellaneous tools.
    The army corps engineer park carries tools for 2,640 men.
    The army park contains tools for 1,576 men.

CHAPTER X.

PART II.

AVIATION.

The aeronautic services in Italy are now (1913) being reorganized, and the outline given below must be considered as *provisional*.

An inspector of aeronautic services is being formed with headquarters at the Ministry of War. There are three distinct branches under him—the "specialisti" battalion already mentioned (Chapter X, Part I), the aviation battalion, and the manufacturing and experimental branch.

The aviation battalion consists of headquarters, a flying sub-division of two companies and a technical sub-division. The headquarters of the battalion are at Turin.

The flying sub-division carries out the management of the aviation schools and provides aeroplane squadrons for the army.

There will probably be 20 squadrons—12 for the 12 army corps, 2 for the cavalry divisions, and 6 for the fortresses.

The aviation schools at present are at Somma Lombarda, Aviano, Pordenone, and Mirafioro near Turin.

There is a school for pilots from both the army and navy at Bracciano.

The establishment of the aviation battalion is as follows :—

	Officers.	Under Officers and N.C.Os.	Privates.
Headquarters	38	21	18
1 Company	4	18	113
Total Headquarters, 2 Companies	46	57	244

The administration of the aviation battalion is carried out by a committee of a lieutenant-colonel or major junior to the commanding officer, two captains, and the paymaster, and the battalion has also a small committee for technical engineer matters.

The staff of the manufacturing and experimental branch consists of a director (lieutenant-colonel or major of engineers), six officers, and a medical officer and four civilian assistants.

The branch has an office and an air-dock for experimental purposes at Vigna di Valle, near Rome, and various subdivisions.

The company of mechanics from the "specialisti" battalion is permanently attached, both for technical duties and for discipline, to this branch.

The administration of the branch is carried out by a committee consisting of the director, two engineer officers and two accountants.

*Details of Aeronautic Services.**

(a) *Organization of an aeroplane squadron.* A squadron will consist of 7 aeroplanes—4 in reserve for mobilization, and 3 for exercises and instruction. There will be a commander, 4 pilot officers, 4 observing officers, and 30 other ranks, including mechanics. The transport will be motor car for personnel, 1 workshop motor lorry, 1 motor lorry for stores, oil, petrol, and spare parts and 2 motor tractors.

(b) *Types of aeroplane* machines and numbers.

There are at present about 10 private firms now established in Italy, and a government competition for the purpose of encouraging local industry has been instituted.

Some 60 aeroplanes will be purchased in the near future, some in the open market, and some under limited tenders to Italian or other firms working in Italy.

The machines at present in use are mostly French—Farman, Blériot, Nieuport and Breguet—and there are a few Bristol machines (English) in use which are highly spoken of.

In March, 1912, there were over 70 machines in Italy and in Libya.

---

* Details of organization of the Aeronautic Services must be considered as provisional, as the types of aeroplanes, and the transport, have not yet been decided on.

The squadrons with army corps will be monoplanes, and the remainder biplanes.

(c) *Types of dirigibles* and numbers.
The following dirigibles are allotted to the army :—

P 1. For experiments } The motor is a Clement-Bayard 100–120 h.p.
P 2, P 3 } For instructional work

P 4, P 5 }
Dimensions as for the other P machines, but fitted with two F.I.A.T. motors.

In still air they have attained a speed of 65 km. an hour.

The P type have a cubic capacity of 4,350 cubic metres and a crew of 4 men.

The P 4 and P 5 have been constructed owing to the success of this type in Libya.

They are cheaper than the M type, costing £10,000, have a life of 7 years at a cost of about £7,000 for repairs, and can remain 15 hours in the air at a maximum speed of 64 km. an hour, and 30 hours in the air at 45 km. an hour.

M 1. Was only completed in 1912.

Semi-rigid. 12,000 metres cubic capacity.

The dirigible is 82 metres long, 17 metres broad.

The car is 16 metres long, 2 metres broad, is made of steel and covered in, with a hollow steel raft at the base to enable the car to float, and there is a crew of 8 men.

The engine power consists of 2 F.I.A.T. 200 h.p. motors. Speed 70 km. an hour.

Radius of action. 1000 km. at a height of 1000 km.

Armament. 2 machine guns, 2 bomb-throwing tubes, and a pneumatic tube for use against aircraft.

M 2. Type similar to M I., but with 4 100 h.p. Wolseley engines. The dirigible will be ready in April, 1913.

M 3, M 4 } Under construction.

A Parseval airship has recently been bought (9,600 cubic metres), and the Citta di Milano, Forlanini type, is also under construction—cubic capacity 12,000 cubic metres.

(d) *Docks* for dirigibles.

The docks for dirigibles are at Campalto near Venice, Verona, Milan, Ferrara and Bracciano.

(e) *Dirigible* units are organized for war only.

Dirigibles will be based on their own docks, or else will fly from dock to dock.

In case of war abroad, a special organization will be improvised.

Dirigibles can be repaired in their own docks.

(*f*) *Telephotography* and *air maps.*

Telephotography has been thoroughly studied in Italy, and has reached a high standard.

A good air map of Italy should have been completed by the end of 1912.

Scales of ground in plan on a scale of 1/10,000 and also 1/2,500 have been produced by telephotography, and have proved very accurate.

(*g*) *Aviation* courses.

There is an annual courses for officers in dirigible work which lasts 1 year.

There are two aviation courses annually for officers, and two for non-commissioned officers, each lasting 3 months.

A pupil must make 3 figures of 8 at a height of 50 metres to obtain a first certificate.

A military pilot must have the first certificate, must make a cross-country flight of 100 kilometres at a height of 500 metres, and must be able to strip and re-assemble both aeroplane and engine.

(*h*) *Badges* worn in uniform.

Officers of the aviation battalion or officers attached wear the uniform of their original regiments, with a cap badge of two crossed rifles and a motor screw surmounted by a royal crown. Officers with the first pilot's certificate wear a badge of a gilt eagle on the sleeves of their coats.

Officers with the second pilot's certificate wear the same badge surmounted by a royal crown.

(*i*) i. *Extra duty pay* for aviation duties. All officers taking part in exercises or experiments five kilometres from their ordinary stations receive extra pay on a scale in accordance with the distance from their stations. Under officers, corporals, and privates similarly employed receive 5*d.* and 2½*d.* respectively.

ii. *Officers or civilians* who carry out flights either in aeroplanes, dirigibles, or balloons receive extra pay as follows:—

		s.
Aeroplane flights ...	⎧ Half-hour	4
	⎨ Half-hour to two hours ...	8
	⎩ Over two hours	16
Dirigibles	⎧ Less than one hour... ...	4
	⎨ One hour to three hours ...	8
	⎩ Over three hours	16
Free balloon flights	⎧ Less than two hours ...	4
	⎨ Two hours to six hours ...	8
	⎩ Over six hours	16

Under officers and head civilian workmen receive half, and corporals, privates, and civilian workmen one quarter of the above rates.

If several flights are carried out on the same day the rates are granted for the longest flight.

iii. Officers and civilians attached to aeronautic stations, docks for dirigibles, or aviation camps receive extra duty pay at the following rates :—

Field officers	2s. 6d. daily.
Other officers and civilians belonging to the artillery and engineers	2s. 1d. ,,
Others attached	1s. 8d. ,,

(k) *Portable Sheds or Hangars.*

(i) For dirigibles.

The hangar used for dirigibles, P type :—

Height, interior measurements	...	23·63 metres.
Width ,, ,,	...	26·8 ,,
Length	...	68·4 ,,
Weight	...	90,000 kilogs.
Resistance to wind	...	100 kg. to the square metre.
Time of construction	...	100 days.
Time of erecting	...	4 ,,
Men required for erecting ...	...	80 to 100.
Railway trucks for transport	...	40.
Price	...	£7,200.

A strengthened type was used in Libya.

(ii) For aeroplanes.

The Italian portable shed or hangar used in Libya, and on manœuvres in Italy, weighs 20 to 24 cwt.

It covers an area of 13 metres by 14 metres (42½ ft. by 46 ft.).

Height for monoplanes :—
    3 metres (9·9 ft.) at the sides.
    5·5 metres (18 ft.) at the centre.

Height for biplanes :—
    4 metres (13·2 ft.) at the sides.
    6·5 metres (21·4 ft.) at the centre.

Any one of the four walls can be removed, and it can be pitched in one hour.

Price £140.

(*l*) Headquarters of aeroplane squadrons and aeroplane parks :

The 12 army corps squadrons will be stationed as follows :—
    1, Cuneo ; 2, Turin ; 2, Busto Arsizio ; 1, Treviso ; 1, Padua ; 2, Rome ; 2, San Maurizio ; and 1 Ferrara.

There will be 2 parks with workshops—1 at San Maurizio and 1 at Gallarate.

CHAPTER XI.
MACHINE GUNS.

Organization.—The present organization was adopted in 1909, when it was decided to form a machine gun section in each regiment of cavalry, infantry and bersaglieri, and in each battalion of "alpini".

Each section consists of two machine guns, with pack equipment. Each section is commanded by a subaltern and is attached to a company or squadron for administrative purposes; for training it is directly under the orders of the regimental colonel.

The bersaglieri machine gun section belongs to the cyclist battalion and is equipped with motor cycles.

Each gun has 5 motor cycles—2 for the gun and mounting, and 3 for the ammunition.

For tactical purposes a section is divided into a manœuvring subsection and a reserve subsection.

Peace Establishment.

	Officers.	R. & F.	Animals.
Infantry	1	14	4
Cavalry	1	17	23

The war establishment of a section is as follows :—

	Officers.	Rank and File.		Animals.		Vehicles, 1 S.A.A. Cart, 1 Baggage Cart.
		Firing Detachment.	Transport Attendants.	Riding.	Pack or Draught.	
Infantry or 'Alpini':—						
Manœuvring subsection	1	10	11	—	10 (1)	—
Reserve subsection	—	—	5	—	6	2 (2)

(1) 12 mules in the "alpini."
(2) In the "alpini" one of these vehicles is replaced by 4 mules, the other is a specially constructed Alpine ammunition cart.

* Each battalion will be provided shortly with a machine gun section.

The cavalry machine gun section consists of :—

Headquarters.
1 officer.
2 N.C.Os.
1 trumpeter.

Manœuvre Subsection.

Firing Detachment.
2 N.C.Os.
12 men.
20 horses.
4 boxes S.A.A.

Echelon for S.A.A.
1 N.C.O.
3 men.
8 horses.
4 boxes S.A.A.

Reserve Subsection.
1 S.A.A. cart.
1 baggage wagon.
1 N.C.O.
3 men.
7 horses.
1 spare horse with pack saddle.
8 boxes S.A.A.

The machine gun now in use is the Maxim, made in Italy, but a lighter pattern of machine gun is being introduced.

Ammunition.—The ammunition used for the machine guns is identical with that used for the infantry rifle.

Ammunition is carried in three echelons as follows :—

Units.	M.G. Sections.	Amm. Columns.	Army Corps Artillery Park.	Total Rounds.
"Alpini"	26,460	18,140	—	44,600
Cavalry	13,000	Not yet fixed.	—	13,000
Infantry	19,000	35,316	17,000	71,316

Armament.—The firing detachments are armed with the regulation carbine, the transport attendants with a revolver.

CHAPTER XII.

THE INTENDANCE, THE COMMISSARIAT AND ADMINISTRATIVE CORPS.

The Intendance.

The intendance is composed of combatant officers belonging to the Staff Corps.

Peace.

In peace time it has few executive duties, but it forms a division of the Chief of the Staff's department, and consists of the following three sections :—

- (a) *Intendance Office.*—(All matters connected with the general working of the administrative services.)
- (b) *Transport Office.*—(Movements of troops in peace and war, the preparation of mobilization time tables, &c.) In war, this division becomes the General Direction of Transport.
- (c) *Accounts Office.*—Officers destined for intendance duties on mobilization assemble annually at the War Office to be posted in their duties in case of war. A proportion of artillery, engineer, medical, veterinary and commissariat officers are attached to the intendance division.

War.

In war the head of the intendance division at the War Office will usually become Intendant General. This officer is responsible for the whole of the administrative services both at the front and on the lines of communication. He is in constant relations with :—

1. The Supreme Commander.
2. The War Office, as regards the replenishment of stores and the keeping open of the lines of communication.
3. The army intendants, who make their demands through him.

The offices of the intendant general and of the army intendants are controlled by the chiefs of the staff to those officers.

The two offices have the following branches :—

Intendant General.	Army Intendant.
General direction of transport and lines of communication.	Army transport and lines of communication direction.
Medical section.	Army medical direction.
Commissariat section.	Army commissariat direction.
General telegraph section.	Army telegraph commission.
Postal section.	Army postal direction.
Veterinary section.	Army veterinary direction.
Artillery section.	Army artillery direction.
Engineer section.	Army engineer direction.
Carabinieri section.	Headquarters of carabinieri.
Representative of the Red Cross Society.	Delegate of the Red Cross Society.

The working of the administrative services in war is shown in Appendix IX.

The Commissariat Corps.

The commissariat is responsible for the supply clothing for the provision of barrack furniture, and for the services, and general administrative services of the army.

Organization and Peace Establishment.

In 1910 various modifications were introduced into the organization of the Commissariat, by the provisions of which the commissariat is organized as follows :—

(1) An inspectorate.
(2) 12 commissariat directions.
(3) 12 supply companies.

Commissariat Directions.

There is one direction to each army corps region. The director is responsible to the army corps commander for the general working of the commissariat corps, for the control of all supply establishments and commissariat personnel, for the distribution of supply companies among the various supply establishments, and for preparation for mobilization. He is responsible to the War Office for making contracts for the supply of food and forage, and for the collection of information as to the supply potentialities of the army corps region. The work of the directions is decentralized to divisional commissariat sections and to local supply offices.

Commissariat Officers.

The following is a list of the commissariat officers:—

Inspectorate.
    1 Inspector of Commissariat Services (Major-General).
    1 Colonel or Lieutenant-Colonel.
    1 Lieutenant-Colonel or Major.

Commissariat Officers.
    12 Directors (Colonels or Lieutenant-Colonels).
    57 Lieutenant-Colonels or Majors.
    142 Captains.

    211

Administrative Officers.
    12 Majors.
    12 Captains.
    61 Lieutenants or Sub-Lieutenants.

    85

Supply Officers.
    12 Majors.
    104 Captains.
    126 Lieutenants or Sub-Lieutenants.

    242

Officers are recruited from among lieutenants of all branches of the service who have been through a two-year course at the Staff College.

The subalterns of the supply companies are recruited partly from subalterns on the supplementary list and partly from company serjeant-majors of the supply companies with not less than one year's service in that rank. There are also 226 attached officers including officers in charge of magazines.

Supply Companies.

There are 12 supply companies, one to each army corps region.

The total peace strength of the commissariat corps in addition to the officers already mentioned is 3,188 non-commissioned officers and men, who form the permanent establishment. To supplement the peace strength a number of men are usually attached to the supply companies from infantry battalions for miscellaneous duties. The companies are of varying strength and include butchers, bakers, millers and mechanics.

War Organization and Strength.

Commissariat Service.

The following organizations are formed in war :—

1st Line *Organizations.*

Groups of Alpine Troops.

Supply Columns.—Each column consists of—
Headquarters.
1 section with pack transport.
1 section with wheeled transport.

Each section has a squad for every company and battery in the group.

Reserve Supply Parks.—Each park consists of—
Headquarters.
2 sections with wheeled transport.

Each section has headquarters and a squad for every company and battery.

Field Bakery Sections.—Each section consists of—
Headquarters.
1st echelon with 6 pairs of ovens on pack transport.
2nd echelon with 1 ration of flour and salt with pack transport.
3rd echelon with 3 rations of flour and salt in wheeled transport.

The 2nd and 3rd echelons have squads for each company and battery of the group.

Infantry and Cavalry.—Infantry divisions, cavalry divisions, the army corps troops, and army troops have *supply sections*, with cattle parks attached.

Each army corps has a *supply column,* a *supply park,* and a *field bakery* section.

A *Supply Column* is composed of—

Headquarters.
3 squads for each division.
3 squads for the corps troops.

A Supply Park consists of—

Headquarters.
The personnel necessary for supply services.
2 squads for each division of the army corps and for the corps troops.

Field Bakery Section with *Weiss* ovens.

A bakery section consists of—

Headquarters.
A squad with 10 ovens for each division of the army corps, and a squad with 5 ovens for corps troops.

2nd *Line Organizations.*

Each army has the following 2nd line organizations :—

Advanced Supply Depôts.

An advanced supply depôt is composed of—

Headquarters.
Transport.
2 squads for each cavalry and infantry division forming the army, and 2 squads for each set of corps troops.

Each squad carries 1 flour ration, 1 supplementary ration, and 1 oats ration. Hence the advanced supply depôt carries 2 days' rations for the army.

Advanced Army Bakeries.

These have a varying number of bakery sections with field ovens, and also without ovens, using the local resources.

These sections make bread, principally baked hard, for the supply columns and issue it through them to the supply sections.

Army Cattle Parks.

Each park consists of—

Headquarters.

1 section for each infantry and cavalry division, and set of corps troops, and Alpine group (if forming part of the army).

Each section has 6 days' meat ration on the hoof.

Reserve Army Supply Parks.

A reserve army supply park consists of—

Headquarters.

Personnel for supply services.

3 squads for each infantry and cavalry divisions and each set of army troops.

1 squad for any army troops not included above.

The park carries approximately, 3 days' preserved meat, biscuit, *pasta risone*, salt, coffee, sugar, tobacco and oats for the army, one day's rations in each squad.

The table in Appendix V shows the number of rations carried by the 1st line organizations and gives details of the rations.

Corps of Administration.

The duty of the corps of administration is to keep the accounts of units, institutions and establishments.

In order to carry out these duties administrative officers are attached in due proportion to all units and establishments, and to the commissariat directions.

The administrative corps consist of 356 officers, as shown below :—

1 Colonel.
9 Lieutenant-Colonels.
24 Majors.
149 Captains.
173 Subalterns.

These officers are recruited—one quarter from the 2nd lieutenants on the supplementary list, and three quarters from company serjeant-majors of all arms with not less than one year's service in that rank. To qualify for admission to the administrative corps, officers must pass an examination in general knowledge and in special subjects connected with administrative duties. The company serjeant-majors must have passed successfully through a course on book-keeping and administration.

UNIFORM.

Commissariat Corps.

Parade Dress.

Forage cap as worn by the infantry; the badge in the forage cap is a light blue star with a circle in the centre enclosing a cross. A light blue piping is worn on the forage cap. Tunic similar to that worn by the infantry; the collar has a light blue edging; the men wear the number of their company worked on the shoulder.

Trousers dark blue: light blue stripe for officers, light blue piping for men.

Lace and ornaments, gold.

Corps of Administration.

Tunic dark blue, turned-down collar with light blue edging, and black velvet facings.

Trousers grey, with blue stripes.

Lace and ornaments, gold.

Service Dress.

As worn by infantry, with distinctive badges, and with the grey drill service dress; supply companies have blue shoulder straps.

Armament.

Non-commissioned officers and men of the supply companies carry side-arms only.

CHAPTER XIII.

THE MEDICAL AND VETERINARY CORPS.

The Medical Corps.

In peace times the establishment of the Medical Corps is as follows :—

    1 Lieutenant-General.
    3 Major-Generals.
  26 Colonels.
  36 Lieutenant-Colonels.
 113 Majors.
 314 Captains.
 280 Lieutenants.
3,652 Non-commissioned Officers and Men.

The medical officers are divided into two classes—the regular army medical officers and the medical officers on permanent furlough — who form a reserve of medical officers.

Candidates for commissions in the regular army go through the Army Medical School at Florence. As certain privileges are granted to men of the first category who are medical students if they pass through this school and serve for 1 year with troops or in a military medical establishment, almost all medical graduates in Italy go through this school and are available on mobilization as complementary or reserve medical officers.

Organization.

Peace.

The technical administration of the army medical service is carried out by an Inspectorate at Rome, which acts as a Medical Advisory Board. Each army corps has a medical direction, under a colonel, who commands the army medical troops in the command and is responsible to the army corps commander for all medical details. The remainder of the army medical corps is distributed among the hospitals, army medical school, and other establishments, and to regiments.

The treatment of sick in peace time is carried out in regimental and garrison sick rooms, hospitals, convalescent depôts, and military bathing establishments.

The number of men allotted to various units varies according to local conditions.

War.

The distribution of medical services in the field is given in the table facing page 197. The medical arrangements are under a surgeon-general, and each army in the field has a director of medical services. Each army corps has a principal medical officer who commands the field ambulance of army corps troops and co-ordinates the medical services of the army corps. Each division has an administrative medical staff officer on the divisional staff.

The following organisations are formed :—*Army* : 2 field hospitals, 1 advanced, 1 central and 1 pharmacy depôt, and Red Cross units. *Army Corps* : 1 field hospital, 1 infantry ambulance, and Red Cross units. *Infantry Division* : 2 field hospitals and 1 infantry ambulance, and Red Cross units. *Cavalry Division* : 1 cavalry ambulance.

The collection and distribution of sick and wounded follow the practice of other continental armies.

Full details of the Italian Medical Service are given in Part V, Handbook of the Medical Services of Foreign Armies, 1911.

The approximate establishment of the various medical units in war is as follows :—

Unit.	Officers.	Rank and File.		Horses and Mules.	2-Horsed Vehicles.
		Medical Corps.	Transport.		
*Cavalry Ambulance	4	28	13	15	6
*Infantry Ambulance	8	228	21	32	16 (3)
*Mountain Ambulance	6	139	60	62 (2)	16
Field Hospital— 50-bed	6	30	4	27	3
Field Hospital— 100-bed (1)	7	27	8	13	7
Field Hospital— 200-bed	9	40	18	24	9
Hospital Train	4	45	—	—	—

* Officers include 1 chaplain and 1 quartermaster.
(1) Some additional personnel found by Red Cross Society.
(2) Eighteen pack mules with sanitary stores.
(3) Eight ambulances, each carrying six men sitting or four lying.

Proposed Changes.

Each cavalry and infantry ambulance will have two motor ambulances and one motor cycle.

A motor ambulance carries six lying down and four sitting cases.

Medical Officers attached to Units.

	Peace.	War.
Infantry of the line and Bersaglieri	2 to 3 per regiment.	7 per regiment.
Alpini	1 to regimental headquarters. 1 per battalion	1 to regimental headquarters. 1 per company.
Cavalry	2 per regiment	2 per regiment.
Artillery	2 ,,	1 per "group."
Engineers	2 ,,	3 per regiment.
Mountain Artillery	4 ,,	1 per battery.

UNIFORM.

Officers.

Forage cap, same shape as in the infantry. The corps badge is of white metal with a red cross in the centre.

Tunic, dark blue, turned down collar with crimson velvet patch.

Trousers, dark blue, with stripes of dark crimson. Silver ornaments and lace.

Rank and File.

Similar to infantry, except that the corps badge is a star with a red cross in the centre. A white pompom is worn in the shako with the number of the company in red; a band with a red cross is worn on the arm.

Armament.—The rank and file wear side-arms only.

The Italian Red Cross Society.

The Italian Red Cross Society was founded by Royal Decree in the year 1882. It is organized on a semi-military basis and is closely affiliated to the regular medical service. Enrolment in it exempts from any other form of military service.

The Red Cross Society is a large and influential association which is likely to prove of great assistance to the army in case of war. Its present capital is about £200,000, and it possesses medical plant and stores to the amount of nearly £60,000.

The following is a list of its personnel :—

Members.	Mobile Stations.	Fixed Stations.	Total.
Doctors	980	234	1,214
Pharmacists	164	43	207
Administrative Officers	276	63	339
Accountants	177	57	234
Chaplains	100	23	123
Warrant Officers and N.C.Os.	603	58	661
Clerks	45	2	47
Trained Hospital Attendants	916	79	995
Orderlies with some training	604	30	634
Cooks, etc.	113	3	116

There are also large numbers of Italian ladies who have attended voluntary ambulance courses in various parts of the country and whose names are registered by the Society.

In case of war, the following are the medical units that would be organized by the Society. As far as officers are concerned these units could be mobilized at very short notice :—

War hospitals (100 beds)... 6
   ,,   (50 beds) 42
Wheeled ambulances 78
Hospital trains. Each for 200 sick or wounded 15
Railway medical posts 65
River ambulances 2
Medical store magazines 8

In peace time the most noteworthy work of the Society has been that shown on manœuvres and on the occasions when Italy has been subjected to one of those scourges—earthquakes, epidemics and the like—which periodically occur. During the earthquake at Messina in 1908 the Italian Red Cross established 16 hospitals and despatched a staff of nearly 1,000 doctors and nurses to the scene of the disaster. Though the work done was valuable, it was noticed that the amateur nurses who volunteered their services were not an unqualified success, their enthusiasm being, unfortunately, in some cases only equalled by their ignorance.

Great progress, however, has been made since the Messina earthquake. During the Libyan campaign a hospital ship was fitted out and hospitals established at all the places occupied by the Italian troops. No ladies are now accepted as nurses who have not gone through a prescribed course of nursing at a hospital and obtained a certificate of competency. The lady members of the Society also did good work in seeking out and assisting the indigent families of dead soldiers whose addresses the Ministry of War had been unable to find.

Veterinary Corps.

The Veterinary Corps consists of the following officers :—

1 veterinary colonel.
4   ,,   lieutenant-colonels.
16   ,,   majors.
85   ,,   captains.
107   ,,   lieutenants and 2nd lieutenants.
―――
213 total.

The corps is composed of the following :—

(1) An inspectorate at the War Office.
(2) An office of military bacteriology, which works in conjunction with the veterinary inspectorate.
(3) Veterinary branches in each army corps region.
(4) Veterinary branches in the cavalry school, horse breeding establishments and other special institutions.
(5) The garrison horse infirmaries.

Three veterinary officers are attached to each cavalry regiment, two to each regiment of artillery.

In war time two horse infirmaries are attached to each army corps, each estimated for 150 quadrupeds. The veterinary personnel consists of 3 officers, 74 rank and file, and 6 horses per infirmary.

CHAPTER XIV.
TRANSPORT.

Composition.—The Italian army has no regular transport corps. For transport purposes, the artillery and engineers furnish the following transport companies:—

Active army—
Horse Artillery*	... ...	4 companies.
Field Artillery*	... ...	36 ,,
Engineers	... ...	11 ,,

Mobile militia—
Artillery	... ...	24 companies.†
Engineers	... ...	4 ,,

* At present there are 2 horse and 4 field artillery mechanical transport companies.

† 36 companies will eventually be raised.

Peace Establishment of a Transport Company.

—	Officers.	Rank and File.	Horses.
Artillery	3	90	40
Engineers	3	100 to 110	40 to 54

In peace time the artillery and engineer transport companies are divided among the various regiments, and are employed in training, and in garrison duties.

In time of war the artillery transport companies provide the necessary transport for headquarters staffs, for the various 1st line services and for part of the 2nd line services of the mobilized army (see Appendix IX).

The artillery mechanical transport companies provide part of the 1st line services, and are employed for the rapid re-filling of various services direct from the central parks, such as the clearing of the sick and wounded from the divisional ambulances, the supply of fresh meat to the fighting troops, and the daily supply of cyclist battalions.

The transport of 2nd line services for which no provision is made will be carried out on mobilization by forming auxiliary transport columns, the personnel being provided by men from the cavalry, artillery, infantry, transport of the territorial militia, and men of the second and third category of the territorial militia, and the vehicles or motors by requisition.

It is intended apparently that these transport columns shall have mechanical transport, and carry one days' rations from the advanced posts to the various supply sections with the 1st line. They will be organized by the automobile park.

All animals, harness, vehicles, motor cars, and motor cycles required can be requisitioned in times of emergency.

The engineer companies will supply transport to the engineer staffs and units.

Efficiency of the System in War.—It is doubtful if the above system is likely to promote either rapid mobilization on the outbreak of hostilities or an efficient transport system when the campaign has begun. The expansion which the transport companies will have to undergo on mobilization is out of all proportion to the strength of the peace cadres, and the officers will lack the necessary training and experience. The adoption of mechanical transport may to some extent obviate these difficulties, but on the whole it appears likely that the transport difficulties will prove a serious handicap to the Italian army during the earlier stages of a campaign.

Uniform, Equipment and Armament.—The uniform of the transport companies is the same as that of the artillery or engineer regiments to which they are attached, except that a star is worn on the headdress with the number of the regiment in the centre. The equipment is similar to that of the artillery and engineers.

The transport companies furnishing transport to ammunition columns or parks are armed with 1891 carbine and bayonet. The remaining companies are armed with the sword only.

Motor Cars.

The motors used in Libya were nearly all 25–30-h.p. F.I.A.T. lorries, with pneumatic tyres, and twin tyres for the back wheels. These vehicles can go over almost any rough ground.

Mechanical Transport.

The 6th Regiment Engineers (p. 94) has already one automobile company, and more are being formed, the Horse Artillery has 2 automobile companies at Monza and Mantua, and the Field Artillery regiments at Bologna, Rome, Piacenza and Rivoli have each 1 automobile company.

A census of all four-wheeled motor cars is being taken in Italy with the object of ascertaining the numbers available for military service. The following table shows the proposed arrangements, but it must be considered as *provisional*, and it is doubtful if the arrangements are complete :—

Table showing Motor Vehicles required on Mobilization.

Unit.	Motor Cars.	Ambulances.	Motor Cycles.	Remarks.
Cavalry Division.				
Headquarters	3	—	10	Motor transport for 1st line organizations (p. 197) is as a rule supplementary to the horse transport.
Hqrs., Cyclist Bn.	2	—	11	
Each Co. ,,	1	—	2	
Cavalry Ambulance	—	2	1	
Supply Section	2	—	3	
Infantry Division.				
Headquarters	3	—	10	
Infantry Ambulance	—	2	1	
Supply Section	5	—	2	
Army Corps.				
Hqrs., Cyclist Bn.	2	—	11	
Each Co. ,,	1	—	2	
Infantry Ambulance	—	2	1	
Supply Section	2	—	—	
Army.				
Headquarters	18	—	10	* Numbers vary according to requirements.
Army Intendance	23	—	10	
Automobile Park	*	*	*	

The automobile park is divided into three classes for motor cars—light, ordinary, and those for headquarters of columns. The numbers vary according to the number of units in the army, but the ordinary work is carried out by transport columns already mentioned.

CHAPTER XV.
HORSE SUPPLY.

Census Returns.

The general horse census, taken in 1908, showed the number of horses in Italy to be 906,000.

Peace Requirements.—The peace establishment of horses is over 53,000. About 5,000 are required annually to replace wastage, of which 1,657 go to the artillery.

War Requirements.—It is estimated that the number of horses and mules required on mobilization is about 133,000. Taking the total amount of quadrupeds on a peace footing at 43,000, the number required on mobilization would amount to approximately 90,000.

Quality of Horses.—There has been a surprising improvement in the quality of the cavalry horses of late years owing to the energetic measures taken by the Government, not the least of which has been the importation of thoroughbred stallions from England, which has proved a marked success. The heavy cavalry and some of the lancer regiments are mounted on big horses showing considerable breeding, and they would compare well with the cavalry horses of any army. The light cavalry are mounted on small 14.2 horses of a good stamp, 50 per cent. of which are Sardinians. The artillery horses also show a marked improvement.

Breeding Establishments and Remount Depôts.—The Ministry of Agriculture controls seven stud farms with some 500 stallions, the services of which can be obtained by local farmers.

The Minister of War, in order to encourage the breeding of the coach horse, the type required for field artillery, boards out with well-known breeders, and farmers, young mares, taking them either from remounts bought in the country or abroad. The mares are only lent, and remain the property of the State. The produce is the property of breeder, but the Government has the right of first refusal at a fixed price. After a certain time the mares are withdrawn, and sent to the ranks, or else sold to the breeder and replaced.

Mares are also sold from the remount depôts at a reduced price to breeders, the purchaser paying three quarters and the Minister of Agriculture one quarter of the price.

The *army remount depôts* are at Bonorva (Sardinia), Grosseto (Tuscany), 1st Remount Squadron, Persano (Campania), 2nd Remount Squadron, Paterno section, Porto Vecchio, Palmanova section, Lazio and Fossano, Artillery Remount Section.

The personnel employed at the first six named is :—

Rank.	Bonorva.	Grosseto.	Porto Vecchio.	Palmanova Section.	Persano.	Paterno. Section.	Lazio.
Lieut.-Cols. or Majors	—	1	1	—	1	—	—
Captains	2	2	1	1	2	1	2
Lieutenants	—	2	—	—	2	—	—
Administrative Captains or Lieutenants	1	2	1	—	2	1	2
Veterinary Captains or Lieutenants	4	3	3	1	4	1	2
Overseers	2	3	1	1	2	2	2

A third remount squadron will be formed eventually. Remount squadrons have the same establishment as squadrons of cavalry regiments.

Depôts are commanded by cavalry lieutenant-colonels or majors; captains command the remount squadrons or sections; one or two veterinary officers are attached to each section.

Each depôt has an administrative officer and a staff of superintendents and stable hands.

About 12,500 horses are kept in all at the depôts. They are bought at two, three or four years old and in all cases remain at the depôts until they are rising five. Horses from the remount depôts are issued to the cavalry and artillery only.

Purchase of Horses.—The young horses in these depôts are all bred in Italy, and are purchased by commissions composed of three officers, who buy at prices fixed by the War Office. In addition, the administrative councils of regiments or units are empowered to purchase such horses as cannot be supplied by the remount depôts. The average price paid for a 3-year-old is £28 ; by the time he is fit for service he was formerly estimated to have cost £36 to £40, but according to the Commission of Inquiry the cost amounts to £57 per horse.

Officers' Chargers.—About 1,000 officers' chargers are required every year, and cavalry officers usually buy Irish horses. An annual allowance ranging from £11 to £16 is paid to each officer entitled to a charger ; if the horse has been obtained from the Government the allowance is stopped until the purchase value of the horse has been made up. Prices vary from £100 for a general's charger to £20 for that of a junior infantry officer.

Mobilization Arrangements.—Each commune keeps a register of all animals contained in it. Every army corps region is visited once in three years by a commission, composed of one or two officers and a veterinary surgeon, who check the communal registers and classify the horses and mules as fit for certain branches of the service. On mobilization a commission assembles in each of the 261 zones into which Italy is divided for requisitioning purposes ; animals are chosen, the price is arranged and paid at once, and the animals forwarded to the collecting centres.

Expenditure.—It has been estimated by the Commission of Inquiry that no less a sum than £1,200,000 is spent every year by the Government and by private individuals on the importation of horses into Italy ; three-quarters of these imported horses come from Austria-Hungary.

The expenditure on horse supply in the estimates of 1912-13 was as follows :—

	£
Estimates of the Minister for Agriculture	96,240
Army Estimates	302,000
	£398,240

These sums include the cost of the remount depôts and prizes for the encouragement of horse breeding.

Mules.—There are 330,000 mules in Italy. The peace requirements only amount to 300 mules per annum. In view of the enormous supply available no difficulty is likely to be experienced as regards mule supply in time of war.

CHAPTER XVI.

EDUCATIONAL ESTABLISHMENTS AND COURSES OF INSTRUCTION.

Military Colleges.

There are two military colleges—at Naples and at Rome respectively.

The course of instruction lasts three years.

Boys of from 14 to 18 years of age with certain educational and physical qualifications are admitted.

The instruction given is on the general lines of that given at the Lycée and other similar government establishments. Some military instruction is also given.

Successful students are given diplomas corresponding to those granted in secondary government schools, are admitted without examination to the Military School, and are eligible for the Military Academy and the Naval Academy after passing the entrance examinations.

Cadets 19 years of age may also be appointed sub-lieutenants of cavalry and infantry after serving 4 months as serjeants, and after qualifying under the same conditions as those for complementary sub-lieutenants.

The annual cost of maintenance at the military colleges is £32, in addition to an outfit allowance of £14 and an annual payment of £9 12s. 6d. for miscellaneous expenses.

The uniform worn by cadets resembles partly that worn by officers and partly that worn by the rank and file of the army.

The Military School.

The Military School is at Modena, and is divided into two parts :—

    (a) for cadets.
    (b) for under officers.

(a) Youths between 17 and 22 years of age, with the certificate of the military colleges, or who have obtained certain civil qualifications and have passed an entrance examination, are admitted to the school.

The War Office decide on the numbers for admission annually.

The course of study lasts two years from October 15th.

The subjects taught include military subjects, military history, topography, small arms and artillery, chemistry, practical physics, geography, principles of social science, Italian literature, French, and German (optional).

Practical instruction in gymnastics, riding and fencing, and in the field is also given. Cavalry cadets are given special instruction in equitation.

(b) Under officers of the regular army, bachelors or widowers without children, with 2 years' seniority in their rank, and not over 25 years of age, who are recommended by the Promotion Board, are admitted to the school after passing a preliminary and an entrance examination.

Candidates with civil certificates of matriculation are excused the preliminary examination.

The course of instruction lasts two years.

The subjects taught are similar to those taught to the cadets.

Special instruction in technical subjects is given to under officers who wish to become accountants.

Artillery and engineer under officers desirous of promotion in their own arms also receive special instruction.

Administration of the School.

Students are divided into companies, which are formed into one or more battalions.

Cavalry cadets form a squadron of 2 or more sections.

Under officers form a battalion of 3 companies.

These units took part in the manœuvres of 1911, and this will form part of their training in the future.

Military Academy.

The Academy is at Turin.

Candidates must have the same qualifications as for the Military School, with the addition of passing an examination in mathematics. The course lasts three years. The subjects taught include military subjects—artillery field fortification, small arms, military history, topography, law and geography, physics, chemistry, mechanics, drawing, French, mathematics and various other subjects. Gymnastics. fencing,

(B 10416)

riding and practical instruction, form part of the syllabus. Staff rides are also carried out.

Administrative details are similar to those of the Military School, and students are formed into companies. Three companies form a brigade.

School of Musketry.

The school is at Parma. The permanent small arms committee forms part of it and experiments are carried out there.

The professional education of newly appointed infantry subalterns is completed in the school, and instruction is given to junior non-commissioned officers to prepare them for the rank of under officer, corporal major, &c.

A machine gun course has been instituted recently.

The course for sub-lieutenants lasts 8 months, and serjeants who, after leaving the Military School, are not yet absorbed, can also attend.

The instruction, which is entirely practical, includes military subjects of all kinds, and training in shooting with the rifle.

Cavalry School.

The school is at Pinerolo with a course in connection with it at Tor di Quinto, Rome, for cross-country riding. Every cavalry officer on leaving the military school at Modena attends the school. The course for sub-lieutenants lasts 8 months, and serjeants not yet promoted officers from a want of vacancies are also admitted. The instruction given is in equitation, veterinary services, engineering, telegraphy, and other military subjects.

On completion of the course at Pinerolo, officers and serjeants join their regiments, and subsequently come to Tor di Quinto for a further course of about 12 weeks in two batches, the first from the beginning of October to the end of December, and the second from the beginning of January to the end of March.

In consequence they spend 8 months at Pinerolo, 4 or 7 months with their regiments, and nearly 3 months more at Tor di Quinto.

There are also veterinary courses for training complementary veterinary officers, farriers' courses, machine gun courses, and 3 months' courses for senior cavalry lieutenants where practical instruction, lectures on cavalry subjects, and written papers on general subjects are dealt with.

The Cavalry School also provides grooms and horses for the instruction of equitation in military institutions.

School for Sub-Lieutenants of Artillery and Engineers sent from the Military Academy.

The school is at Turin, under the command of the Commandant of the Military Academy.

There are three courses of instruction :—

(a) *The Regular Course.*—Newly-appointed sub-lieutenants from the Military Academy and complementary lieutenants join the course, which lasts two years. Each arm is taught separately, and the subjects of instruction are technical. Both engineer and artillery officers are taught fencing, riding, and practical exercises. Staff rides and visits to fortifications and military establishments are also carried out.

(b) *The Supplementary Course.*—Newly-appointed sub-lieutenants from the special course of the Military School attend the course, which lasts nine months. Practical training and staff rides form part of the instruction.

(c) *The Special Course.*—This course is only formed when it is necessary to accelerate the supply of officers.

The Army Medical School.

The school is at Florence.

Soldiers of the first category who have delayed their military service to complete their studies at a university, and who have obtained honours in medicine and surgery, are admitted before becoming sub-lieutenants. The course lasts seven months, and consists of instruction in technical and military subjects, and in riding and fencing.

School of Gunnery.

Station, Nettuno.

The school is under the command of the IXth Army Corps for discipline, and under the Inspectorate of Artillery for technical subjects.

Senior lieutenants and captains attend the school. They receive instruction in directing artillery fire with the special object of making the system of training throughout the artillery uniform. New systems are practised, and also experimented on. At the school itself there is a detachment in addition to the permanent staff. When the school is not open, the personnel are under the orders of the Inspectorate of Artillery.

The details in connection with the various courses are decided on by the War Office.

Field artillery courses usually take place at the practice ground at Nettuno, fortress artillery courses at Nettuno, or at Bracciano, coast artillery courses either partly or wholly in a coast fortress.

The Staff College.

The college is at Turin, and is under the 1st Army Corps for discipline, the Chief of the General Staff for training, and the War Office for the entrance and dismissal of officers under instruction.

Not more than 100 officers are admitted by competitive examination. Before competing at the entrance examination officers must have been specially recommended by the Promotion Board, and have served four years in the cavalry or infantry, and three years in the engineers and artillery of which at least two years must be with their units.

The subjects for examination include written tests in military subjects, and history, and oral tests in military subjects, geography and French; candidates may also be examined in German, English or Russian.

The course lasts three years, each annual course lasting nine months. In the intervals officers are attached for two and a half months to arms other than their own.

At the end of the third year most of the officers are sent to take part in the manœuvres attached to headquarters, brigade headquarters, and to the umpire staff.

The instruction given in the school includes military history, tactics, logistics, organization, geography, topography, communications, arms and fortifications, general history, social science, French, German, or English, fencing and equitation.

Student officers also take part in field exercises near Turin, and visit military establishments, railway stations, and artillery practice grounds. Officers who complete the course successfully receive a certificate of fitness from the War Office.

Those considered fit for probation on the general staff are attached to the headquarters of the general staff. This probation lasts one year—six months at headquarters and six months at a local headquarters.

At the end of the year their fitness for the general staff is decided on.

There is also a course for officers desirous of being appointed commissariat captains. Lieutenants of infantry, cavalry, artillery and engineers, are admitted after an examination. The number is decided on by the War Office. The course lasts two years.

In the interval between the first and second year students serve at the headquarters or sections of the commissariat, either locally or at manœuvres.

At the end of the two years they serve one month in the field, and are attached for two months to the intendance section of the general staff.

The course of instruction includes administrative military subjects, political economy, chemistry, commercial geography, French, German or English, equitation, fencing and cycling.

Miscellaneous. Courses of Instruction.

Minor military courses of instruction comprise a fencing school at Rome for sub-officers, the syllabus for instruction including instruction in fencing, sword exercises, gymnastics and military subjects, courses for soldiers desirous of becoming complementary sub-lieutenants held under the direction of certain army corps, which last 6, 7, or 9 months, varying according to the arm of the service desired, and courses for serjeants held in selected regiments.

The other courses of instruction are :—

    (a) Annual course of telephones and signalling for officers of coast and fortress artillery which lasts 20 days.

(*b*) Railway courses at Turin, Venice, Ancona and Naples for non-commissioned officers of cavalry, artillery, infantry and engineers.

    The courses last 50 days, 15 of which are devoted to technical instruction.

(*c*) Automobile courses for junior officers which last from 30 to 50 days.

(*d*) Topographical course for artillery officers which lasts three months.

(*e*) Telegraph and telephone course for officers of cyclist companies of Bersaglieri, and for cavalry pioneers, which lasts four months.

(*f*) Courses of instruction in military engineering for infantry which last two months and take place at the School of Musketry.

(*g*) Courses for pioneers of cavalry at the Cavalry School which last three months.

(*h*) Courses in each army corps command for captains to test their fitness for promotion which last one and a half months.

(*i*) In addition there are various technical courses for artillery officers.

CHAPTER XVII.
FINANCE AND PAY.
The Budget.

The Italian Army Budget is divided into two parts—the ordinary expenditure, and the special expenditure.

The First Part (*ordinary expenditure*) is sub-divided into three headings.

(i) General expenses, which include the pay of the officials civil and military at the War Office, postal and office expenses, allowances of various kinds, the publication of the official gazette, and official military journal.

(ii) Pensions and annuities.

(iii) Cost of the Army.

The principal sums expended under these various headings in the budget for the year 1912–13 are as follows :—

	£
Sub-heading (i)	149,736
Sub-heading (ii)	1,561,760
Sub-heading (iii)	12,040,776
	13,752,272

The principal sums expended under (iii) are approximately the following :—

	£
General Staff, pay of	130,668
Infantry officers } „ rank and file }	1,518,312
Cavalry officers } „ rank and file }	249,832
Artillery officers } „ rank and file }	487,156
Engineer officers } „ rank and file }	135,604
"Carabinieri"	1,049,266
Military schools, pay of staff	94,492
Equipment and stores	1,009,020
Bread, rations	671,348
Forage	1,198,772
Artillery material and establishments	484,244

(25 lire = £1.)

The Second Part (*extraordinary expenditure*) consists of sums voted for certain expenses which are divided over a number of years or which will not occur again.

The amount voted for 1912-13 is £3,150,000.

The principal sums under this heading are :—

£		
400,000	for	buildings.
378,416	„	fortresses.
126,976	„	coast defence artillery.
80,000	„	purchase of horses for artillery, cavalry and machine guns.
596,800	„	small arms and ammunition.
757,776	„	new field artillery.

Pay and Pensions of Officers, Non-Commissioned Officers and Rank and File,

PAY OF OFFICERS.

Rank.	Pay.	Special Allowance.			Personal Allowance.
		Carabinieri.	*Army Medical Service.	Veterinary Service.	
	£				£
General	600	—	—	—	120
Lieut.-General ...	480	—	—	—	—
Major-General ...	400	—	—	—	—
Colonel	320	88	16	—	—
Lieut.-Col. (after 5 years' service)	280	84	12	—	—
Lieut.-Col. ...	240	84	12	—	—
Major (after 5 years' service)	220	76	12	—	—
Major	200	76	12	—	—
Captain (after 10 years' service)	192	60	12	8	—
Captain (after 5 years' service)	168	60	12	8	—
Captain	160	44	8	8	—
Lieut. (after 15 years' service)	144	44	8	8	—

* Medical officers of the following ranks receive additional pay also :—Lieut.-General £96, Major-General £48, Colonel £24, Lieut.-Colonel £24.

PAY OF OFFICERS—continued.

Rank.	Pay.	Special Allowance.			Personal Allowance.
		Carabinieri.	Army Medical Service.	Veterinary Service.	
Lieut. (after 10 years' service)	140	44	8	8	—
Lieut. (after 5 years' service)	112	44	8	8	—
Lieutenants ...	96	44	8	8	—
2nd Lieutenants	80	32	8	8	—
Bandmaster ...	80	12½	—	—	—

(25 lire = £1.)

Allowances.—Officers are entitled to various allowances, travelling expenses, &c. The following are instances :—

Sub-lieutenants on first appointment receive £12 for equipment.

Officers promoted to mounted corps from the rank of sub-officer are given £24 for equipment.

Officers quartered at Rome receive £1 monthly when not provided with quarters or lodging allowance.

Officers holding certain appointments receive special sums of money, *e.g.* :—

	£	s.	d.	
Chief of the Staff or Commander of an Army Corps	192	0	0	yearly.
In a Lieutenant-General's appointment	96	0	0	,,
In a Major-General's appointment	48	0	0	,,
Commander of a regiment ...	36	0	0	,,
Military Attaché, for expenses	160	0	0	,,
Officers of Alpini and Mountain Artillery	1	10	0	monthly.

(For aviation allowances, see Chap. X, Part II.)

	In Camp.	On the March.
Travelling expenses daily—	£ s. d.	£ s. d.
General	0 8 6	0 10 0
Lt.-General or Major-General Commanding a Division.	0 7 6	0 8 6
Lodging Allowance—		
Army Corps Commanders ...	—	24 0 0 monthly.
Lieut.-Generals or Major-Generals Commanding Divisions.	—	12 0 0 ,,

Office Expenses.	*Office.*	*Fuel Allowance.*
Army Corps Commander ...	£80–88	£12–£40 yearly.
Division	£56–80	£16–£28.
Brigade of Infantry or Cavalry...	£16	—

In war time officers are entitled to an outfit allowance, additional daily pay, free ration daily, and office expenses.

Pensions of Officers.—Pensions are granted to officers under certain conditions.

The table below shows the amounts payable.

Rank.	Minimum 25 years' Service.	Maximum.
	£	£
Lieut.-General	176	320
Major-General	140	288
Colonel	112	224
Major	102	141
Captain	74	138
Lieutenant	66	77

* War pensions are granted to both officers and other ranks on a scale which depends on the severity of the injuries sustained. The amounts paid are only given to pensioners who receive less than £120 yearly, and the total sum allowed must not exceed the sum.

Pensions for widows and orphans under age are granted at the rate of one-third of the amount of that for officers. If, however, the officers have died as the result of their military service their widows or orphans are entitled to half the pensions which such officers would have received.

Pay of N.C.Os. and Rank and File.

Regular Army—

	Daily Rate.
	s. d.
Warrant officer (" Maresciallo capo ")	4 9
,, ,, ,, maggiore ")	3 11½
,, ,, ,,	3 2
Serjeant-major	2 4½
Serjeant	1 7

The above receive 3d. extra for every four years' service, until a "maresciallo maggiore" receives 5s. 6d., a "maresciallo capo" 4s. 5d., and other serjeants 3s. 6½d. daily. Warrant officers are stopped 2d. and other serjeants 1½d. daily for clothing.

	s. d.
Pioneer corporal-major	0 5
Drummer-trumpeter, corporal-major	0 4
Corporal-major	0 4
Engineer, musician, trumpeter, drummer, corporal	0 3
Corporal and farrier	0 2½
Lance-corporal, pioneer, trumpeter, drummer	0 1½
Soldier	0. 1

	Dismounted.	Mounted.
Carabinieri—	s. d.	s. d.
Senior warrant officer	4 9	5 1
Chief ,, ,,	3 11½	4 3½
Warrant officer	3 2	3 6
Serjeant ("brigadiere"), musician or trumpeter	2 10½	3 2½
Lance-serjeant ("Vice brigadiere")	2 6	2 10
Lance-corporal, musician, and trumpeter	2 0	2 3
Carabiniere	1 10	2 1
Recruit carabiniere	0 3½	0 4

Senior warrant officers receive 3d. daily for every 4 years' service, until a maximum of 5s. 6d. a day is received.

Extra duty pay is granted to certain grades, e.g. :—

		s.	d.		s.	d.	
Engineers, railwaymen	...	1	7	daily.			
Under officer, mechanics } or	...	1	2½	,,	2	0	by night.
Corporal, electricians }	...	0	9½	,,	1	7	,,
Under officers, motor drivers	...	1	2½	,,	} When driving.		
Corporals ,,	...	1	0	,,			
		0	7		} When on duty in a garage.		
		0	4½				

Soldiers employed on engineer works :—

				d.	
1st class	...	...	...	1	per hour.
2nd ,,	...	...	...	¾	,,
3rd ,,	...	...	...	½	,,

Pensions and Reserve Pay.

Under officers * on the *reserve* receive for every year's army service 1/40th of the rate of pay of the last year's army service.

Under officers on retiring after 20 years' service receive a pension calculated at the rate of half the pay received during the last year's army service in addition to 1/50th of this sum for every year's service between 20 and 30 years.

Under officers and rank and file of the "Carabinieri" who go to the reserve after 15 years' "Carabinieri" service receive reserve pay at the rate of 1/40th of the pay received during the last year's service for every year's "Carabinieri" service.

Pensions for the "Carabinieri" are similarly granted at the rate of half the pay received in the 20th year's service, plus 1/5th of the amount arrived at. For every year's service between 20 and 25 years the pension is increased by 1/25th of the pay received in the 20th year's service.

---

* Under officers, definition of, *see* p. 49.

CHAPTER XVIII.

INSTRUCTION AND TRAINING.

Annual Course of Training.

The training of the Italian army begins on the arrival of the annual contingent of recruits.

The army corps commanders decide on the dates when the higher training of units is to begin, and the regimental commanders then make their own arrangements for the training of their units.

The whole programme of training has to be completed before the dismissal of the senior contingent on unlimited furlough which takes place in September.

In the interval between the dismissal of the old contingent and the arrival of the new one, a period of from 3 to 6 weeks, instructors are prepared for their duties in connection with the training of the recruits, and subjects, which have for one reason or another not received sufficient attention during the training season, are dealt with.

Under ordinary circumstances the recruits' course of training, which is always carried out in the company, squadron or battery, lasts for the following periods :—

Infantry and Engineers ...	8 to 12 months.
Artillery	4 to 6 months.
Cavalry	5 to 6 months.

Details of the Course.

Infantry, General Instructions.—The system is based on thorough instruction by the company commander. The syllabus includes company, battalion and regimental training, marching, outposts and reconnaissances, entraining and detraining, field fortification, and musketry ; and theoretical instruction is given in military law, discipline, care of arms and ammunition, hygiene, pay, and other military subjects.

The soldier carries his full equipment, which weighs 56½ lbs., at all marches, field training, and musketry.

The route marching of recruits is carried out by companies and is progressive up to 20 kilometres (12 miles) per day. When the recruits have joined the ranks, route marching is carried out regimentally and is progressive up to from 20 kilometres (12 miles) to 30 kilometres (18¾ miles) a day.

Bersaglieri units carry out marches of from 25 kilometres (15⅝ miles) to 40 kilometres (25 miles) a day.

In every garrison officers are encouraged to give lectures on military subjects, and a free discussion takes place after each lecture.

War games, and tactical exercises with skeleton forces, are often held.

Inspections are made by battalion, brigade, and regimental commanders.

Musketry.—Musketry forms one of the most important parts of the annual training, and great importance is attached to fire discipline and fire control.

The number of rounds per man allowed annually is :—

—	Ball.	Blank.
Infantry and bersaglieri	160	66
Alpini	170	72
Discipline companies	100	18
Educational establishments, infantry	18	—
Reserve men of the army, or mobile militia called up for training for the 1st line	42	36
Ditto ditto for the territorial militia	30	24
Ditto subsequently recalled for training	30	18
Recruits of medical and supply companies	36	18

Units taking part in the manœuvres make up to 42 rounds blank in addition per man.

The general distribution of these rounds is as follows:—

	Rounds.	Range.
I. Recruits' course	72	100 to 200 metres.*
II. Classification course—		
Individual fire	66	300 to 450 ,,
Collective fire...	60	450 to 1,000 ,,
Rifle meeting, field firing ...	Local authorities determine the number of rounds to be used.	

* 100 metres = 109·4 yards.

Winter Training ("Tiro di perfezionamento")—54 rounds, 18 rounds of which are included in the number of rounds per head allowed annually, and 36 rounds are allotted on the basis of the men actually carrying out the practice.

The targets in use consist of plain bull's-eye targets and figure targets. Thirty-six rounds of the recruits' course and 6 rounds of the trained soldiers' course are fired at a bull's-eye target.

The remainder of the individual and collective firing takes place against figure targets which consist of dark blue figures on a khaki ground, each figure having a white bull's-eye 30 centimetres (11·8 ins.) in diameter with two additional rings for inners and outers. These targets are about the same size as those used in the English army.

Rapidity of fire is practised, and the rate varies from 6 rounds a minute in the recruits' course to 12 rounds in 90 seconds in the classification practices. Field firing is practised and rifle meetings are also held. Captains and subalterns fire individual practices and a revolver course.

Judging Distance.—Judging distance correctly is the particular duty of officers below the rank of major, under officers, and non-commissioned officers.

The training is progressive, and non-commissioned officers are taught map reading and the use of range-finders in connection with it.

Men in the ranks are pointed out the various distances of the targets on the ranges but receive no particular training.

The instruction is given in two periods—from November to May, both inclusive, and from June to October.

Competitions are held and prizes given, a sum at the rate of 8s. per company being allotted to the battalion commander.

Cavalry, General Instructions.—The cavalry units are trained on similar lines to the infantry units. The course of training includes instruction in fitting saddles, equitation, individual training, mounted and dismounted, reconnaissance, and cavalry duties generally. Officers and non-commissioned officers receive special instruction in breaking remounts and in fencing. Squadron officers are responsible for all details in connection with the training of their men.

Marches are progressive, beginning at 25 kilometres ($15\frac{5}{8}$ miles) daily and increasing up to 80 kilometres (50 miles) daily for several consecutive days.

The theoretical training of officers, and inspections, are carried out in the same way as in the infantry.

Musketry.—Eighty-four rounds ball and 50 rounds blank per man are allotted for the annual musketry course, and 40 rounds ball and 24 rounds blank for each person armed with the revolver.

Units taking part in the army manœuvres can draw extra blank ammunition at the rate of 24 rounds per carbine and 12 per pistol.

In the recruits' course 24 rounds at 100* metres range are fired.

The annual course for trained soldiers consists of the classification course, individual and collective field firing, classification course with the revolver, and competitions with rifle and revolver.

Individual firing is carried out from 100 metres to 450 metres, and collective firing from 250 metres to 1,100 metres.

Judging distance is taught on the same lines as in the infantry but the distances judged are slightly greater.

Two competitions in each squadron are held annually, in April and in June, and the regimental commander has a sum of money at the rate of 16s. per squadron for prize money.

Artillery.—The annual course of instruction is arranged so that the new recruits are ready to take part in the annual gunnery practice.

---

* 100 metres = 109·4 yards.

145

Marching is carried out once a fortnight, and the distances are progressive—up to 35 kilometres (22 miles) for dismounted men, 45 kilometres (28 miles) for field batteries, and 50 kilometres (30¼ miles) for horse batteries.

Rapid marches are also practised.

The course of training varies in the different branches of the arm but the following subjects are common to the whole of the artillery:—

Musketry, individual, section, company, battery, and brigade training, gymnastics, outpost and reconnaissance duties, transport of material by road or rail, field fortification, camps, and hygiene. Officers go through courses of riding and fencing.

The Minister of War, on the recommendation of the Inspector of Artillery, makes arrangements for the annual gunnery courses, and decides on the nature of the practices and the number of rounds to be fired.

In 1909 the number of rounds allowed was as follows:—

BATTERIES.

		Field.			Horse.		Mountain.
		87 B.	75 A.	75 Mod. 1906.	75 A.	75 Mod. 1906.	70 A.
Number of rounds allotted for artillery practice in 1909.	Shrapnel	200	—	25	—	25	—
	Steel	—	25	—	25	—	25
	Practice	—	175	—	175	—	275
	Shell	—	—	25	—	25	—
	Practice Rounds	—	—	150	—	150	—
	Blank	60	60	80	60	80	60

In 1913 the following number of rounds was allotted for fortress artillery:—

                                                87   Other Machine
                                          Calibre. Guns.   Guns.

Each company of regiments 6—10 ⎫ 50 ⎫ 130   600
    „   fortress company   ... 3—5 ⎭ rounds ⎭

Each regiment, 1, 2 and 4 ... 60 rounds of various calibres.

War Games and Lectures, Field Training and Manœuvres, Staff Tours and Army Manœuvres.

Lectures, War Games, and Staff Tours.—All officers are expected to have a general knowledge of army questions, army organization, and of proposed improvements. Lectures are held from time to time in the garrison towns, and at these lectures free military discussions are encouraged.

War games are also played under a director who has two umpires to assist him, one for each side.

Staff tours are carried out by army corps or divisional commanders, and by cavalry brigade commanders for cavalry officers.

Artillery and engineer officers also carry out special staff tours.

Staff tours on a larger scale are carried out by the Inspector of Cavalry for higher cavalry commanders, and by the Chief of the General Staff for officers of the general staff, both at headquarters and on the staffs of army corps.

The staff tour of the Chief of the General Staff usually takes place on one of the northern frontiers of Italy, and the movements of units smaller than brigades are not considered.

Field Training, and Local Manœuvres.—Field days take place in the different garrisons all the year round and mixed forces are employed as much as possible.

Local manœuvres are used for completing the training of troops who do not take part in the army manœuvres. They are carried out at the same time of year as the army manœuvres, except in Sardinia where they are held in May and June.

The Chief of the General Staff receives the proposals of army corps commanders or inspectors of the various arms and then decides on the scale of these manœuvres.

Army corps or lesser units with a proportion of cavalry and artillery may be employed against each other; or the troops may be engaged with a marked enemy.

Frequent rest days are advised so as to give the directing officers time to hold conferences and to prepare the schemes for the following days.

Army Manœuvres. — Army manœuvres take place in August or September, but they are dispensed with in some years on the ground of economy.

The area selected is usually some part of Northern Italy, such as Lombardy, Venetia, or the basin of the River Po.

The scheme is prepared by the general staff, and operations are continuous as a rule except for rest days.

Umpires are employed with each detachment, and their decisions are final.

Certain conventional signs are used, *e.g.*, artillery opening fire on cavalry unfurls a white flag about three feet square, and displays a red flag of the same size when firing against infantry. If a marked enemy is used, a red flag denotes a company of infantry, a white flag a squadron of cavalry, and a yellow flag a battery of artillery. Similar rules are in force in local manœuvres.

In 1911 the army manœuvres were held in the triangle Turin-Vercelli-Alessandria, from August 22nd to August 29th.

Two armies, each consisting of two army corps, a cavalry division of two brigades, and corps troops of one regiment bersaglieri, one cavalry regiment, and one regiment field artillery, were employed.

Each cavalry division had a battalion of bersaglieri cyclists and a group (two batteries) of horse artillery.

CHAPTER XIX.

FORMATIONS AND TACTICAL TENDENCIES.

Infantry Formations.

The Section.—The section of a company consists of one officer, two to four serjeants commanding squads and from 24 to 60 corporals and privates. It is divided into two, three, or four squads, each from eight to 15 men strong.

In close order a section moves in line or in column of fours.

In open order movements are carried out on much the same lines as in the British infantry. Rifles are carried at the trail, signals are used, and extensions are usually carried out at the double.

In opening fire the section commander gives the object, the range, and the command "Fire." Each man then begins to fire independently paying due attention to his position, the visibility of the target, &c.

If the firing becomes too rapid and ammunition is being wasted, section or squad commanders stop the firing with the whistle.

In ordinary cases the section commander gives the command "Cease fire" when desired, and the squad commanders repeat the command when the section is at open order.

The Company.—The company consists of four sections. The ordinary close order formations are:—

In line.
In line of section columns in fours, sections being at six paces interval ("plotoni affiancati").
In company columns, sections at six paces interval in line.
In column of route.

Instructions for Firing.

In close order the captain of the company usually gives the range and points out the target. In extended order he points out the target and leaves the section commanders to give out the range and regulate the firing.

The Battalion.—There are four companies in a battalion. The ordinary formations in close order are :—

Column, companies being in line of section columns at 10 paces distance.

In double column, two companies being in the front line and two in the second line, the distance and the interval between each company being 10 paces. Companies are in line of section columns.

In line of company columns. All four companies are in one line at 10 paces interval between companies, companies being in line of section columns.

The Regiment.—The regiment, which consists of three battalions, is arranged in one or more lines according to the ground and the object in view. Battalions are in one of the formations already mentioned and for choice in double column.

The Brigade.—In brigade movements the two regiments of the brigade are drawn up, and movements are carried out on similar principles. The intervals between battalions, and the distance between lines in both regimental and brigade drill, are 30 paces.

Machine Guns.—The machine gun section of a regiment follows in rear of the last company of the battalion or of the regiment it is attached to.

In double column or in lines of columns it remains behind the left-hand company of the double column or of the line of columns.

Cavalry Formations.

The Troop.—The troop consists of one leader, two squads with an equal number of privates, and a serrefile with a strength of from 12 to 16 files.

In close order the troop moves in column of route or in line, and in open order in "loose column" ("frotta") or in "groups extended in line" ("stormi").

In "loose column" the rank and file form a single group behind their leader and as close to him as possible.

In "groups extended in line" the men are split up into five or six groups, each consisting of three, four or more men, and can when so disposed occupy the front of two, three or four troops.

The troop can also move in the "independent advance," in which the men when ordered break off independently at the desired pace from any formation and go separately to the place chosen, and on the command rally, followed by an indication of the formation which the commander desires to re-assemble the troop, the men gallop up and take their proper places behind their leaders.

The charge is carried out in line in close order and when extended the troop may be in groups extended in line or in exceptional cases in loose column.

Non-commissioned officers are placed on the flanks of the squads in the front and rear ranks.

Blank files are left in the rear rank which must not, however, have less than half the number of the men in the front rank.

The Squadron.—The squadron consists of a commander and four troops, and two serrefiles, usually the squadron serjeant-major and the quartermaster-serjeant.

The formations in close order are:—

In Column—column of route (in fours or in file)
 —close column—open column.
In Line—line.

Close Column consists of the four troops, each in column o route, on the same alignment, with two paces interval between troops.

Open Column.—The same formation as close column but with troops at deploying interval.

Line.—The four troops are in line without any intervals between troops.

In open order there is only one formation—the squadron extended with each troop disposed into groups extended in line.

The intervals between groups are decided by the commander. The sections are about the same distance apart as the groups in a section.

The independent advance and the rally in the squadron are carried out in the same way as in the troop.

The Regiment.—The *regiment* consists as a rule of the staff and five squadrons.

It may be manœuvred in close order, or part may be in close order and part in open order.

In close order the regiment is in line when the squadrons are on the same alignment, and in column when the squadrons are one behind the other.

The formations in *line* are :—

Mass.
Line of Columns.
Deployed Line.

In *mass* the squadrons in close column are on the same alignment with an interval of 10 paces.

In *line of columns* the squadrons in open column are on same alignment with an interval of 10 paces, and in addition the space occupied by the frontage of a troop, between each squadron.

In *deployed line* the squadrons in line are placed on the same alignment with an interval of 10 paces between squadrons.

In *column* the formations are :—

Column of route in which the squadrons in sections or half-sections follow each other.

Column of squadrons, in which the squadrons follow each other in close column.

Double column in which as a rule the regiment is arranged in two parallel columns of squadrons, one of two squadrons and one of three squadrons, with an interval of 15 paces between squadrons.

The Brigade.—The brigade usually consists of the staff and two regiments.

When working independently, a horse artillery battery and a cyclist detachment may be allotted.

The brigade may be formed in *column* or in *line.*

In *column of route, column of squadrons,* and in *double column* there is a distance of 15 paces between regiments.

In column of masses regiments follow each other at a distance of 160 paces.

In line the formations are :—

Line of masses—the regiments in mass are formed on the same alignment with an interval of 20 paces between regiments.

Line of columns—the regiments are formed on the same alignment in line of columns at an interval of 20 paces in addition to the frontage of one troop.

Line deployed—the regiments are formed in deployed line at an interval of 20 paces.

The Division.—The division consists of the staff, two cavalry brigades, one cyclist battalion, and one group of two horse artillery batteries.

The division can be formed in line or in column.

In column.—In *column of route,* in *column of squadrons,* and in *double column* the brigades follow each other with the regiments in corresponding formations.

In *double column,* the brigades follow each other with the two regiments side by side in column of squadrons.

In *column of masses,* the brigades follow each other with the regiments in mass one behind the other.

In *column of line of masses* the brigades follow each other with the regiments in mass on the same alignment.

In line.—In *line of masses* the brigades are formed on the same alignment with the regiments in mass.

In *line of column of masses* the brigades are on the same alignment with the regiments in mass formed one behind the other.

In line of columns and in *deployed line* the regiments are all on the same alignment in line of columns or in deployed line.

Exercises in Dismounted Action.

The squadron is the unit for dismounted action.

It is divided into dismounted men, led horses, and if only part of the squadron dismounts, mounted support.

Dismounting is always carried out by entire troops.

In the dismounted action importance is laid on the principles of fire and movement, and the result is the means by which a decision is sought by a bayonet charge after the necessary fire preparations.

Artillery Formations.

The Battery.—The battery consists, as a rule, of six guns divided into three sections, and the wagon detachment of 12 wagons.

Formations :—
  In line.
  In column.
  In line of columns.
  In action.

In line the interval between guns varies between 5 paces at close interval and 22 paces at full interval, with the wagons at 10 paces distance.

In column the distance between guns is 4 paces. If marching in two columns with the wagons on the flank of the guns there is an interval of 28 paces between the two columns.

In line of columns the formation consists of the sections of the battery, each in column of route, on the same alignment. The intervals between the sections in open line of columns is 44 paces and in closed line of columns 7 paces.

The distance between guns and wagons is 10 paces.

In action the interval between guns is usually 22 paces. The wagons are 10 paces behind the guns.

The gun limbers and remainder of the wagons are about 200 paces in rear.

The Brigade.—A brigade of artillery is made up of two or three batteries of field artillery or two batteries of horse artillery.

The formations of a brigade are :—

In line at close interval or at full interval.
In line of columns.
In column.
In action.

In line the interval between batteries is 35 paces, the batteries being either at full interval or at close interval.

In line of columns the batteries in column are on the same alignment, and the interval between batteries varies from 35 paces at close interval to 145 paces at full interval.

In column the interval between batteries is 20 paces.

In action the brigade is arranged in line or in echelon, according to the ground, with intervals and distances to meet each particular case.

Infantry Tactics.

No fixed general rules are laid down, but the principles of co-operation, mutual support, and the general objective in view, must be remembered.

Formations are to be suited to the ground, and extensions must not be too wide in the attack. On the defensive wider extensions are allowed so that more troops may be available for the decisive counter-attack.

The Offensive.—At the beginning of the action the troops are arranged in depth with the leading units extended, and forming successive lines, while the other units are in denser formations.

As the action progresses, one thick powerful firing line is built up.

Fire is opened when the effect of the enemy's fire prevents a further advance. The order to begin firing is given by the commanders of the leading battalions.

The subsequent advance is by "bounds" or rushes, which should be unexpected and at irregular intervals of time.

At first it should be possible for whole companies to advance in this way. When this is no longer possible, sections and squads advance alternately, and finally the firing line pushes forward by a few men, or even by one man, at a time, in each squad advancing. The importance of fire assisting movement is clearly laid down.

Reinforcements are sent to the firing line on the orders of superior commanders, but if loss is being suffered the reinforcements go forward to the firing line without waiting for further orders.

If the fire fight does not force the enemy to retire, the assault determines the fate of the day. In carrying this out, one single thought should be in the minds of everyone taking part in it. "*Push on, push on always and at any cost,*" and the troops are taught that those who hesitate are lost.

The Defence.—Defensive positions must be chosen so that the offensive can be undertaken at the suitable moment.

The troops on the defensive are usually divided into two parts—one to occupy the position and one to reinforce the firing line either wholly or partly, or else to counter-attack.

Fire is opened when a suitable target is offered.

Cavalry Tactics.

General Principles.—Cavalry is said to be the arm for swift movements, for rapid action and for surprise.

It can carry out reconnaissance work of all kinds and must also co-operate on the battlefield with the other arms.

Cavalry fights mounted with shock tactics and dismounted with fire tactics.

The defensive must only be employed in cases of absolute necessity, and the maxim that *cavalry defends itself by attacking* must always be remembered.

Simplicity in action is insisted on, and fixed rules are not made. The experience and instinct of the commander must guide him in every situation.

The charge is the principal act of every engagement. This is preceded by the preparatory stage, the approach or manœuvre, and the deployment. After the charge follow the melée, the pursuit, and the rally.

Considerations which affect these movements are the tactical situation at the time, the hostile numbers and dispositions, the moral and physical condition of the enemy, and the ground.

Preparatory Stage.—In the approach, and preparatory stage, column of route, double column, or some similar formation such as column of squadrons is adopted.

During these stages the commander, by means of personal reconnaissance and from the information he receives, forms an idea of the general situation and if possible assumes a position of readiness, and decides on his plan of action. He may order such a formation as line of columns, and then line, or deployed line.

The Charge.—As the distance between the adversaries grows smaller, the pace is gradually quickened, and finally when a short distance from the objective the charge is delivered with the utmost vigour.

The melée which follows the charge is an individual struggle at close quarters, and victory will be gained by those who fight hardest and have the most complete control of their weapons and their horses.

The Pursuit.—The pursuit will be at first irregular, but will gradually become organized and will follow some regular tactical plan.

If the commander sees any opportunity of effecting a surprise during the preliminary movements of the attack, he must abandon all idea of manœuvre and send his troops in any formation and in the most direct line against the enemy.

Cavalry against Infantry.—An attack against unshaken infantry, well provided with ammunition, and well posted, is recognized as a desperate affair, but against shaken infantry, short of ammunition, or infantry engaged with infantry at short range, or preparing to charge, an unexpected cavalry charge may produce a great effect.

If possible the advance should be under cover, but in any case the attack ought to be made against the flanks or rear of the infantry. Formations are of secondary importance, but it is absolutely necessary for the commander to seize the psychological moment for delivering his charge.

Cavalry against Artillery.—Artillery in position should be attacked on the flanks. The artillery escort of cavalry must be charged in close order. Artillery on the march, or when limbering or unlimbering the guns, is most vulnerable. Once the battery is reached, the limbers should be seized so as to drive away the guns when captured.

If the guns cannot be moved, they should be made useless by taking away some essential part.

General Instructions.—A very free hand is given to subordinate commanders, such as squadron leaders, in carrying out the duties assigned to them. This is particularly the case in the broken and wooded country which is common in Italy.

The following points are considered of special importance :—

Every formation must be considered as part of a well considered plan of manœuvre. Those units which cannot act mounted may employ fire action and produce excellent results when this is combined with the mounted action of other units.

Units when separated from one another and without orders must act on their own initiative, and direct their movements for the common end.

Every commander must be inspired with the strongest desire to come into the fight at all costs, and he must be too bold rather than too cautious. The unpardonable crime is to do nothing when there is any possibility of action.

Artillery Tactics.

The artillery with a force must devote all its efforts to co-operate in the general plan.

From the beginning of the action its particular objectives must be those attacked by the infantry belonging to the force.

In a division tactical command of the batteries is entrusted to the commander of the divisional artillery and he distributes his batteries in accordance with the divisional orders.

The same procedure is followed in an army corps with the corps artillery.

Before coming into action batteries should be assembled in places from which they can occupy the necessary positions for opening fire easily, and without being seen by the enemy.

In action batteries must fire as much as possible suddenly and simultaneously so as to develop irresistible fire effect.

The long range of modern weapons and the ease with which the target can be changed facilitates rapid and powerful concentration of fire on objectives which have been chosen.

Careful decentralization of command and good means of communication are necessary to carry these measures out effectively.

Economy of ammunition is considered most important, and one of the first duties of an artillery commander is to see that arrangements are made for the ready supply of ammunition to his batteries.

The infantry when attacking must not wait for the result of the artillery duel. Sooner or later the advance of the infantry will attract the enemy's artillery and the artillery must at this moment make every attempt to facilitate the infantry advance.

After the hostile artillery has been silenced, artillery will fire on the hostile infantry, and in the absence of good targets the fire should be directed on the areas which are probably occupied in this way. As the action progresses batteries must be prepared to move forward so as to support the attacking infantry.

Heavy artillery should be made use of from the beginning of the fight, and if any artillery is left in reserve at all, it must be the most mobile.

General Tendencies.

The Italian regulations discuss three kinds of battle—the unexpected, the encounter battle, and the deliberately prearranged battle.

The unexpected battle is not described and is only referred to as a warning. The encounter battle is dealt with at some length.

It is considered as coming half-way between the unexpected and the prepared battle, and in it the question of time is of great importance. Two theories are advanced—that of the general advanced guard, and that of a deliberate deployment on a premeditated plan.

In the first case the situation is cleared up by making use of a considerable portion of the force, and then, when he has gained information in this way, the commander of the force decides on the plan he means to adopt.

In the second case, owing to the size of modern armies and the difficulties of drawing correct conclusions even from the action of a general advanced guard, the commander deploys his forces on a deliberate plan and attempts to impose his will on the hostile commander.

The first case necessitates dispositions in depth with the object of penetrating the hostile front. The second implies an approach march on a wide front, preparatory to outflanking the enemy on one or both of his flanks.

No precise rules as to which form of battle should be used are laid down.

A deployment in depth, however, is insisted on, and it is pointed out that the commander must not limit himself to the preliminary dispositions in a battle, but that he must be able to keep control over his forces throughout the action.

The modern ways of communication in some ways make this task easier nowadays than it has been in the past.

The commander may decide the fate of the day by a suitable use of the troops in reserve under his command.

Finally the Italian regulations are very decided in insisting on the necessity of a strong and determined commander, and on the great superiority of the offensive over the defensive.

CHAPTER XX.

RECONNAISSANCE, PROTECTION, MARCHES, CAMPS, BILLETS AND BIVOUACS.

GENERAL REMARKS.

The Italian regulations deal very fully with the services of reconnaissance, protection, marches and camping arrangements.

As a general rule the instructions resemble those given in Field Service Regulations, Part I, with the exception that the defensive line of the outposts is usually the line occupied by the supports.

Reconnaissance and Protection.

Great importance is attached to the services of reconnaissance and protection and no precaution which can render them more efficient must be omitted. At the same time it is pointed out that these services are exhausting to the troops and that the numbers so employed must be restricted.

No trumpet calls or drums must be used by troops marching or in camp under service conditions

Reconnaissance.

Reconnaissance is ordinarily carried out by cavalry and by cyclists.

Distant reconnaissances may be pushed forward several days' march in advance of the armies; *near reconnaissances* are made within a radius of two or three hours' march by cavalry and cyclist units attached to columns, and *reconnaissance for shorter distances* are the duty of infantry patrols, who must keep in close touch with the troops they are covering.

When troops begin to deploy, the reconnaissance for the fight takes place.

All arms assist in this; the cavalry watch the hostile flanks and rear, and the other arms reconnoitre the front and their own flanks, and keep up communication with each other.

There are no fixed rules for carrying out reconnaissances, but at the same time every patrol or detachment sent out on such duties must be given a definite task and must be allowed a free hand in carrying it out. Once the contact with the enemy is obtained, it must be kept day and night.

Information to be of value must reach headquarters as soon as possible, and the commander of any patrol must not go beyond a distance from which he can send back his messages.

Cavalry Reconnaissance.

Cavalry attached to army corps or to infantry divisions, carry out the special duties of reconnaissance in front of the advanced guards.

As reconnaissance takes time, patrols should be sent out before the main body marches.

These reconnaissances must not be pushed forward too far, as the information must be sent back in sufficient time to be acted upon, and communication must be maintained with the advanced guards. At the same time the cavalry commander must still have liberty of action to carry out his own task.

The main body of the cavalry is not necessarily compelled to use the road which the column is marching on, but the general direction of the march must be maintained.

In principle, the cavalry advance is by bounds from one important position to another.

Cyclists detachments are most useful and at night may replace cavalry altogether, but generally speaking they should be used as fighting units.

Reconnaissances by the Other Arms.

In columns of all arms local reconnaissances are best carried out by infantry, who push forward patrols from the advanced guard or even from the main body.

Officers, or selected N.C.Os., on bicycles or motor cycles, can be usefully employed either in local reconnaissance or on particular duties.

Cyclists must be used for the transmission of news whenever possible.

The duty of patrols is to examine the ground so that the units which send them out cannot be surprised, to drive back hostile patrols, maintain touch with the enemy when encountered, and give information.

Engineers should be used for reconnaissances which require technical skill, such as reconnaissances of streams, fortified positions, etc.

Captive balloons are capable, under favourable conditions, of being used to reconnoitre over a radius of about five miles.

Dirigibles and aeroplanes can be used for both tactical and strategical reconnaissances, but officers carrying out such reconnaissances must be in close communication with the higher commanders and must know their intentions.

In general, all units must keep in touch with each other and must inform each other the results of their reconnaissances.

It is particularly important that artillery should let the other arms know the result of its observations.

Protection.

All troops whether halted or on the march must parade for their immediate protection with suitable detachments, such as advanced, flank, or rear guards, and outposts.

In mixed forces the service of protection is the special duty of the infantry.

Protection on the March.

No fixed rules are laid down for the sub-division of a force on the march, but the following example is given for a regiment or brigade of infantry without other arms :—

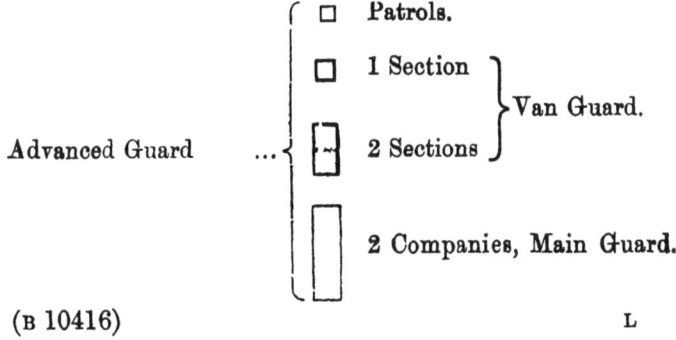

Main Body   ... ...   2 (or 5) Battalions.

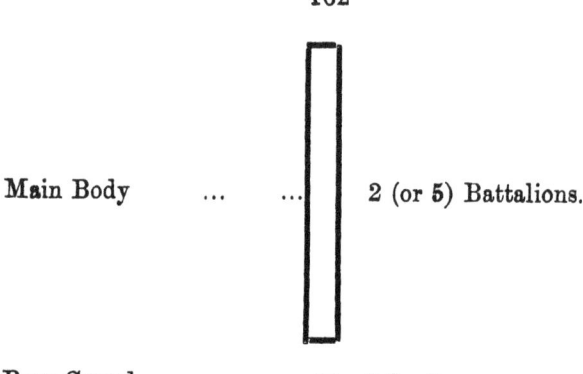

Rear Guard   ... ...   1 Section.

The distances between units vary according to circumstances, the essential point being that each body of troops can support those in front without at the same time becoming involved prematurely in the action.

With forces greater than a regiment a squadron of cavalry should be employed.

Rear guards in retreats are the same as advanced guards reversed, but should as a rule be stronger in cavalry and in artillery than advanced guards. Whole units must, if possible, be always used.

The units entrusted with the protection of the columns on the march carry out the same duties during halts, but if the halts are long the main body may also have to send out patrols or observation posts.

Outposts.

The duties of outposts are to give proper rest to the troops covered by them, to obtain information if in touch with the enemy, and to give the commander of the force time to make his plans if attacked.

Infantry is considered very suitable for the work, and cyclist detachments may be used as mobile reserves which can be easily moved to threatened points.

Not more than one-third of any force should be employed on outpost, but in many cases the outposts may be very considerably reduced in numbers, by placing detachments on the line of resistance and watching the lines of approach with posts.

Cyclist detachments, owing to their mobility, only require the simplest forms of outposts.

The ordinary division of outposts is as follows :—
  Outpost Reserves—
  Supports.
  Piquets.
  Sentries.
  Observation posts.
  Patrols.

Outpost reserves must be near enough to the main body not to be overwhelmed before they can be supported but not so near as to compromise the dispositions of the commander of the forces. .

Supports must be placed on similar lines as regards the reserves.

Piquets must be in good positions for observation, able to communicate easily with the supports, and placed if possible on some well defined natural line such as a road, ridge, hedge, river, etc. .

Three or four piquets are usually found from each support, and they are numbered from right to left.

Picquets consist of one non-commissioned officer and four or five men by day and a complete squad by night (8 to 15 men).

Each piquet finds one or two sentries, who should be able to see without being seen.

Sentries have rifles loaded and bayonets fixed, leaving their packs with the piquet.

The remainder of the piquet put down their rifles and packs, but must not light fires, put up shelter huts, or make a noise.

The commander of the piquet is generally responsible for the duties of his post and for sending back important information to the supports.

Piquets are changed every six to eight hours.

Supports are formed of complete sections, and in important places may consist of companies.

Their strength should be double the strength of the piquets detached from them at night.

They should be easy to approach, out of sight of the enemy, and in good defensive positions. When necessary they are entrenched.

(B 10416) L 2

The commander of the support must know the positions of the reserve, and the supports on each side of him.

The men may put down rifles and packs, put up tents, or shelter in out-houses or verandahs, and may cook.

A guard of about a squad is posted to keep communication with the piquets.

Supports are relieved every 24 hours.

Outpost Reserve.—The strength of the outpost reserve should not be less than the total strength of the supports.

If artillery and cavalry are allotted to the outpost troops, they remain as a rule with the reserve.

The transport necessary for the supply of the outposts remains with the reserve unless it is sent back to the main body.

The troops may encamp or bivouac in out-houses, etc., and a place of assembly must be determined on in case of alarm.

General Control of the Outpost Area.—The commander of the force may divide the line into sections, each with its own commander and troops.

These sections are numbered from right to left, and must be arranged so that important communications are not on the flanks of any section.

Observation posts may be posted in towers or any places from which there are good views. If pushed far beyond the outpost line, these posts should consist of cavalry, or if possible of cyclists.

The commander of the column, during the march if possible, issues the orders for the posting of the outposts.

These orders include :—
Information on the situation.
Position of main body.
Position of G.O.C.
Line to be held by outpost troops.
Distribution of troops, and their commander.
Means given for communication (cyclists, motor cyclists, motors, cavalry detachments and telephones).
Direction of the probable attack of enemy.
Reconnaissances ordered in front of the outpost line.
Method of dealing with inhabitants who wish to pass through the line.
Hour of relief of outposts.
Supply arrangements for men and animals.

While the outposts are being posted the advanced guard covers them from attack.

Outposts must be changed in silence, and as a rule after the dinner hour.

In case of serious attack, piquets fall back on their supports, who either withdraw to the position chosen for defence or remain on their ground, in accordance with their orders.

The reserve is usually sent up to the position chosen for defence, where it and the supports offer a stubborn resistance.

Flags of truce are dealt with in the same way as in Field Service Regulations, Part I.

March Outposts.—If there is no time to put out proper outposts, march outposts are posted. These consist of supports halted, with outposts put out (*in firmata protetta*) on the roads leading towards the enemy, and outpost reserves, similarly protected, if possible, in the direction of the march.

By night patrols watch the ground between the various supports.

Marches.

Rate of Marching.

Great importance is attached to a regular pace being maintained, and no unit should hurry to regain distances lost.

The rates of marching are :—

Ordinary—
    Infantry ... ... 4 km. (2½ miles) in 50 mins.
    Bersaglieri ... ... 5 ,, (3⅛ ,,) ,, ,,.
Special—
    Infantry ... ... 5½ ,, (3¼ ,,) ,, ,,
    Bersaglieri ... ... 7 ,, (4⅜ ,,) ,, ,,
Ordinary Cavalry—
    Trotting and walking 8 ,, (5 ,,) ,, ,,
    alternately, 10 minutes
    with brief halts
    With trained horses ... 10·5 ,, (6½ ,,) ,, ,,
    Horse Artillery ... ... 10·5 ,, (6½ ,,) ,, ,,
    Field Artillery ... ... 10 ,, (6¼ ,,) ,, ,,
Cyclist Sections—
    In favourable conditions 15 ,, (9⅜ ,,) ,, ,,
    Very favourable conditions 20 ,, (12½ ,,) ,, ,,

Halts.

Short Halts.—A short halt of a few minutes takes place after the first half-hour, and then infantry halts 10 minutes every hour and mounted troops from 10 to 15 minutes every $1\frac{1}{2}$ to 2 hours.

Every company, troop or battery, closes up at these halts.

Cyclist detachments should march 30 kilometres ($18\frac{1}{2}$ miles) in 2 hours without halting.

If the columns are large, halts should take place 10 minutes before each hour and exactly at the hour (viz., 1 p.m., 2 p.m., etc.), and each commander of a unit begins the march again without further orders.

The road must be left clear during a halt.

Long halts should take place as a rule in the second half of a march, and no unit should have less than 1 hour's rest.

Length of Marches.

The following particulars apply to forces not greater than a regiment. As the length of the column increases beyond this, the distance of the march decreases:—

Water bottles must be filled, and animals watered before the march.

If possible N.C.Os. mounted or on bicycles should precede the column and warn the inhabitants of villages to have buckets full of water ready so that troops may fill up their cups without halting.

Ordinary Marches.—Trained dismounted troops on foot are expected to march the following distances for several consecutive days:—

Infantry	25 km.	($15\frac{5}{8}$ miles).
Bersaglieri	30 ,,	($18\frac{1}{2}$,,).
Cavalry and Horse Artillery ...	45 ,,	($28\frac{1}{9}$,,).
Field Artillery	35 ,,	($21\frac{7}{8}$,,).

In mountainous country—

Infantry and Bersaglieri march 5 to 6 hours.
Alpini march ... ... 6 to 7 ,,

Cyclist detachments can usually march 80 to 90 km. (50 to 56 miles) in 6 hours.

Forced Marches.—The best results are obtained by marching for a longer time and not by accelerating the pace.

Small columns under favourable conditions march in 24 hours :—

Infantry	Up to 50 km.	(31 miles).
Cavalry	,, 90 ,,	(56 ,,).
Field Artillery	,, 70 ,.	(44 ,,).
Horse	,, 80 ,,	(50 ,,).
Cyclists	,, 150 ,,	(93 ,,).
Alpini	11 hours' marching.	

Marches of Mechanical Transport.

Automobiles must all keep the pace ordered, and must go slowly and carefully in passing troops on the road.

Columns of automobiles march by sections each of not more than 20 motors, with a distance of 100 metres (109 yards) or more between them.

Sections are divided into sub-sections made up of from two to eight automobiles.

March of Transport.

Transport must never be a hindrance to the movements of troops.

It marches at a walking pace on the right side of the road.

When marching alone, it goes 4½ km. (2⅖ miles) an hour with halts of 10 to 15 minutes every 1½ to 2 hours.

Cavalry transport may follow its main body, alternately trotting and walking at 8 km. (5 miles) an hour.

First line transport (S.A.A. carts, medical carts, and water carts) form part of the column to which it belongs, and marches at its tail.

The remaining transport marches in rear of the column at a convenient distance and rejoins in the evening.

In large forces such as divisions and army corps the transport is divided into :—

(i) *Transport for fighting* (carreggio di combattimento) (medical transport, field hospitals, engineer services, first reinforcement of S.A.A.).

(ii) *Heavy Baggage* (grosso carreggio).—In two echelons, the first containing everything required by the troops daily and the second the remainder of the transport.

Cooking carts march either at the tail of the main column or at the head of the first echelon of the heavy baggage.

In marches, when there is a possibility of meeting the enemy, the first echelon of the heavy baggage follows the troops, and joins them in the evening, and the second echelon marches as a rule a day's march in rear.

March Orders.—Starting points are given and orders issued on the same lines as in Field Service Regulations.

Billets, Camps, and Bivouacs.

The choice of quarters and camps depends on the local conditions, the length of the halt, and the nearness of the enemy.

Bivouacs are only made use of when absolutely necessary.

To facilitate administrative services, the larger commands up to brigades, and supply and medical services, should be billeted.

Billets.

As a rule each army corps is given an area on the line of march in which it halts and obtains food, making use of all the local resources available.

The allotment of billetting areas should be made beforehand on the map, or else advanced parties must be sent on ahead of the troops. Divisions can be placed in these areas one behind the other, or else side by side, in accordance with the suitability of the roads.

In billets, units must not be mixed up more than necessary.

In estimating the accommodation available, a number of men with horses and vehicles in proportion, equal to one and a half times the number of the civil population, can be provided with quarters.

In agricultural districts and in the larger towns three times the number of the inhabitants can be provided with billets.

An average space of ·65 metres × 1·9 metres (2·13 × 6·13 feet) per man and ·9 × 2·9 metres (3 × 9½ feet) per horse should be allowed.

In choosing billets attention must be paid to the following points:—

(1) Well defined limits must be given to separate units.
(2) Infantry must be given the area with most houses, cavalry the most level and best watered area, and officers must be quartered near their men.
(3) Wagons must be parked clear of roads, on hard ground, with easy approaches, and near the unit which they belong to.

Ammunition wagons must be away from houses and away from any danger of explosions.

(4) Every unit must have a place of assembly, easy of access.

(5) Headquarters of the larger units must be in central places.

(6) Medical sections must be in sheltered places with water and good accommodation.

(7) Supply sections must be centrally placed, with good communications, and near the troops.

If suitable buildings are not available, their tents must be used.

The facilities for ingress and egress must be carefully studied.

Camps.

During a march units should camp in the order in which they resume the march on the following day. If possible ground near the line of march, with good approaches, firm, dry, not dusty, undulating slightly, where the rain water runs off easily, with good and sufficient water, not too far off, is to be selected.

The shape of the ground, in choosing a camp, must not be sacrificed to any ideas of symmetry.

Battalions usually camp with the companies in line one behind the other with 15 or 20 paces between each.

N.C.Os. are with their companies.

Behind the men's tents, at 15 to 20 paces distance, are the battalion headquarters, tents of the officers, and the transport men near their wagons and animals.

Kitchens and latrines are placed to leeward and in suitable places.

Batteries camp near the egress of the camp—guns and wagons in *close line*, animals behind the vehicles, in circles, tents of the men further in rear than those of the officers, and the target and the tents of the ponies. Kitchens and latrines to leeward in suitable places.

Bivouacs.

When in bivouac squadrons of cavalry are placed according to the ground. As a rule the horses are tied up in circles, each rank of a troop forming one circle, saddles, equipment and arms 15 or 20 paces away, and the men behind in troops, and then the officers and transport.

Other arms only bivouac when it is necessitated by tactical considerations or when on the field of battle.

Men are placed by units at convenient distances and intervals and sleep by their arms. Horses are tied up in circles: artillery vehicles and transport ready loaded and placed so that they can move any hour of the night. Artillery bivouacs should be covered by infantry.

TABLE SHOWING LENGTH OF UNITS, TIME OCCUPIED IN PASSING A POINT, AND CAMPING SPACE REQUIRED.

Units.	Infantry in fours, Cavalry in fours. Artillery (column of route).		Space for Camp.
	Depth in metres.	Time to pass a point.	
Infantry—			
1 Company	90–100	A company of infantry, squadron at a walk; 2 squadrons or a battery at a trot; 4 squadrons at a gallop; pass a point in 1 min. 20 secs.	Battalions: companies one behind the other, 150 metres breadth by 110 metres depth.
1 Battalion	400–450		
1 Regt. (3 Bns.)	1,300–1,400		
1 ,, (4 ,,)	1,800–2,000		
Cavalry—			
1 Squadron	100–125		Squadrons: 60 metres breadth by 80 metres depth.
1 Regt. (4 Sqdns.)	450–550		
1 ,, (5 ,,)	550–650		
1 ,, (6 ,,)	700–800		
Artillery—			
1 Field Battery	250–300	A battery at a walk passes in 3 mins.	Batteries: 60 metres breadth by 100 metres depth.
1 Horse ,,	300–350		
1 group of 2 Batts.	550–650		
1 ,, ,, 3 ,,	850–1,000		

NOTE.—100 metres = 109 yards (about).

CHAPTER XXI.

PERMANENT DEFENCES AND COMMUNICATIONS.

Land Defences.

The permanent land defences in Italy are distributed amongst the different army corps regions. The following table shows the organization of the principal forts and fortresses and the lines of communication affected by them:—

No. of Corps.	Head-quarters.	Forts and Fortresses.	Communications.
I.	Turin	Bard	On road leading from Little St. Bernard pass to Dora Baltea valley.
		Bardonecchia, Susa, Mt. Cenis, Exilles, Cesana, Fenestrelle.	On roads and railway line over the Mt. Cenis and Dora passes, leading to Turin.
II.	Alessandria	Sampeyre, Vinadio, Tenda.	On the roads leading to Saluzzo, and to Cuneo, from the Stura valley and from Nice.
		Casale and Alessandria.	In the centre of a triangle formed by Turin, Milan, and Genoa.
III.	Milan	Rocca d'anfo	Near the frontier on the Trent-Brescia road.
IV.	Genoa	Nava, Zuccarello, Melogno, Altare-Vado, Giovo, Turchino.	On the roads leading from the Corniche road between S. Remo and Genoa to the central plain of N. Italy.
		Genoa, Piacenza	Important fortresses.

No. of Corps.	Head-quarters.	Forts and Fortresses.	Communications.
V.	Verona	Rivoli, Verona,* Peschiera.*	Trent–Verona road and southern end of L. Garda.
		Mantua.* Legnano.*	On the Mincio and Adige respectively, and along the Venice–Piacenza railway.
		Val Leogra, Arsiero.	Between Rovereto and Vicenza in the valley of the Astico.
		Cismon, Primolano.	In the valley Sugana, on the Trent–Padua road and railway and on the Brenta.
		Asiago	In the zone between the valley of the Astico and the R. Brenta.
		Agordo	In the Cordevole valley, 13 miles N.N.E. of Belluno.
		Pieve di Cadore	At the road junction of the Cortina, Tolmezzo, and Belluno roads.
VI.	Bologna	Osoppo. Mestre, near Venice.	On the R. Tagliamento, barring the Tarvis-pass.
VIII.	Florence	Spezia.	
IX.	Rome	Rome, Maddalena.	
X.	Naples	Gaeta, Capua.	
XI.	Bari	Taranto.	
XII.	Palermo	Messina, Castrogiovanni.	

* The Italian fortress quadrilateral.

In addition to the fortresses already named there are forts at Cividale on the frontier W. of Udine, Gemona, N.W. of Osoppo, Latisana and Cividale on the R. Tagliamento, Chiusa Forte between Pontebba and Gemona, Ceraino near Rivoli, Tonale on the frontier at the head of the V. di Camonica, Bormio near the frontier on the Tirano road, and Tirano. The Austrian frontier between Osoppo and the sea has been strengthened considerably, and there are a number of modern forts and block-houses on all the communications through the Austro-Italian frontier.

Maritime Defences.

Italy is divided into three maritime departments, each under an admiral :—

1st Department.—From the French frontier to Terracina, including Sardinia.
Headquarters—Spezia. First class naval harbour.

2nd Department.—From Terracina to Cape Santa Maria di Lucca, including Sicily.
Headquarters—Naples.

3rd Department.—From Cape Santa Maria di Lucca to the Austrian frontier.
Headquarters—Venice. First class naval harbour and naval arsenal. Mestre is the bridge-head for the military defence of the fortress.

Fortresses which are both naval and military are commanded by naval or military officers, according to the relative naval or military importance of the place.

In either case the commandant has entire control and is responsible for all the defences.

Navy and army share in finding the personnel for coast defences; the navy providing for submarine defences, mine fields, torpedo batteries, searchlights, signalling stations and shore batteries, and the garrison of high level forts being provided by the army.

Communications.

Telephonic communication exists between all forts and detached batteries, and the wireless and other telegraph systems are good throughout the country.

The entire frontier, both land and sea, is patrolled day and night by the Customs Guards ("Guardie di Finanza ").*

Railways.—The railways belong almost entirely to the State, and have been much improved in recent years. Owing to the mountainous character of the country and the cost of construction, a large number of the lines have been made with single tracks.

The more important double-track railways are :—

Turin-Alessandria-Genoa.
    ,,   ,,   Piacenza-Bologna.
    ,, Novara-Milan-Brescia-Verona-Venice.
Milan-Piacenza.
    ,,   Pavia-Genoa.
Rome-Naples.

The coast lines both on the east and west of Italy and all the railways crossing the frontiers are single lines.

Railway lines go to the following places on or near the frontier :—

(i) *French Frontier*—
    Ventimiglia, where the Genoa-Marseilles line crosses the frontier.
    Cuneo.
    Bard.
    Pinerolo.
    Bardonecchia, beyond which the Mt. Cenis route crosses the frontier at Modane.
    Susa.
    Aosta.

(ii) *Swiss Frontier*—
    Varallo.
    Brigue-Domodossola to Lausanne.
    Intra.
    Pino, where the St. Gothard Railway crosses the frontier.
    P. Ceresio.
    Chiasso, near Como, where the Bellinzona Railway crosses the frontier.
    Chiavenna.
    Tirano.

* *See* p. 23.

(iii) *Austrian Frontier*—
Edolo.
Verona to Trent.
Schio.
Arsiero.
Asiago.
Primolano.
Belluno.
Pontebba, where the Tarvis Railway crosses the frontier.
Udine to Trieste.
Cividale.
Cervignano.
S. Giorgio Nogaro.

In addition to the railways there are many light railways and steam tramways in different parts of the country, and the communications in this respect are constantly improving.

Rolling stock though still deficient in numbers is being increased.

Roads.—In Northern Italy the roads are good and numerous; in Central Italy the roads vary from good to indifferent and they are not numerous; and in Southern Italy and in the islands the roads are usually indifferent.

Canals.—Northern Italy has a system of canals suitable for irrigation and for navigation by small craft.

The most important canals are the Canale Cavour connecting Turin with the Upper Po and the Ticino, and the Naviglio Grande connecting the Ticino and Milan.

CHAPTER XXII.

COLONIAL TROOPS.

Italy has colonial forces in Erithrea, Italian Somaliland, Libya, and a small detachment of Carabinieri in China.

LIBYA.

Provisional Arrangements.

The new Colony has only recently been obtained as the result of the Turco-Italian campaign of 1911–1912.

The question of providing troops permanently after the country has been pacified is now occupying the attention of the Italian General Staff.

By a Decree of 7th December, 1911, the following new units were ordered to be formed with the object of forming a colonial army corps :—

Infantry	24 battalions (4 companies each).
Bersaglieri...	3 battalions (3 companies each).
Cavalry	5 squadrons.
Artillery	2 groups field artillery (each of 3 batteries).
	4 groups mountain artillery (each of 3 batteries).
	4 groups of fortress artillery (each of 3 companies).
Engineers	2 battalions (each of 3 companies).

Some details of these organizations will be found in the chapters dealing with the various arms.

Small bodies of native troops were also formed during the recent campaign and, no doubt, developments on these lines will be continued.

Particulars of the proposals as to terms of service, pay, and other matters concerning the colonial army in Libya have not been published and no further information is available at the present time.

ERITHREA.

General Description of Troops.

The colonial troops in Erithrea consist of the following units :—

> Headquarters at Asmara, commanded by a colonel, including commissariat, pay services and veterinary services.
> 1 company carabinieri. (Italian and native.)
> 1 company light infantry (Italian) (Cacciatori).
> 4 native battalions (five-company battalions).
> (3 or 4 more battalions are being formed.)
> 1 native squadron.
> 1 artillery headquarters.
> 1 company artillery (native).
> 2 native batteries (4 guns).
> Transport, engineer, medical services, and a permanent military tribunal.

The depôt for the colonial troops is at Naples.

Composition of Units.

Carabinieri Company.
> 3 officers } Italians.
> 57 other ranks
> 150 other ranks, native.
> 96 horses and mules.

Light Infantry Company.
> 3 officers.
> 118 other ranks.
> 3 officers' chargers.

Native Battalion.
> *Headquarters.*
> > 4 officers } Italians.
> > 4 N.C.Os.
> > 11 privates, natives.
> > 10 horses.

(B 10416)

Each Company.
3 officers, Italian.
150 other ranks, native.
9 horses.

Total Five Company Battalion.
19 officers.
4 N.C.Os.
761 other ranks.
20 officers' horses.
4 N.C.Os. „
37 transport animals.

Native Squadron.
2 officers } Italian.
3 N.C.Os. }
60 other ranks, native.
65 horses and mules.

Native Artillery Company.
70 officers. } Italian.
23 N.C.Os. }
260 other ranks, native.
7 horses.

Native Battery.
3 officers } Italian.
7 N.C.Os. }
135 other ranks, native.
94 horses or mules.

The total numbers approximately of the military forces in the colony are :—
150 officers and civilian employés.
700 other ranks.
4,000 to 5,000 natives.
900 animals.

Recruiting for the Colonial Troops.

Italian officers and other ranks are obtained from volunteers of the regular army. If sufficient volunteers are not forthcoming, the deficit is made up by detailing the necessary numbers.

Terms of service are from two to four years in the case of officers, and for two years for other ranks, renewable every two years up to the age of 32 (30 for n.c.os.). N.C.Os. should have 2 years still to serve, and the rank and file are chosen from recruits with not more than 4 months service. Most of the n.c.os. and men are transferred from the regular army, but they may come from the reserve provided that they have not left the colours more than four years.

Native soldiers are recruited by voluntary enlistment in the colony, and a number up to one-third may come from other parts of Africa.

Their engagement may be renewed for further periods of two years.

Pay.—Troops of the regular Italian army receive extra pay during their colonial engagement on the following scale:—

Italian Troops.

Officers.

Ordinary Pay.	Colonial Allowance.	Cost of First Equipment.
£	£	£
60 and under ...	56	8
Over 60 to 80	56	12
„ 80 to 105	64	12
„ 105 to 120	72	12
„ 120 to 160	96	16
„ 160 to 240	96	24
„ 240	96	40

The commandant of the forces receives consolidated pay at the rate of £48 a month and an equipment allowance of £80.

Officers of native troops and engineers receive a special allowance of £36 a year.

Officers mounted in the colony, but who would not be mounted in Italy, receive an allowance of 11s. 6d. monthly.

N.C.Os. and Men.—In addition to their ordinary pay n.c.os. and men receive extra duty pay daily in amounts varying from 2s. to 3d., and extra duty pay annually increasing with every year's service.

For example, the higher ranks of n.c.os. with Italian troops receive about £7, £9 10s. 0d. and £11 15s. 0d. for the first three years, and £22, £24 and £26 similarly if employed with native troops.

Private soldiers receive £4 2s. 6d., £7 4s. 6d. and £10 2s. 6d. for the first three years with Italian troops, and £11 12s. 6d., £14 12s. 6d. and £13 2s. 6d. similarly when with native troops.

In addition other allowances for lodging, furniture and light are given, and daily rations are issued.

Native Troops.

Native troops receive daily pay which includes the cost of their food, lodging and general maintenance.

When campaigning they are issued with about 21 ozs. of flour or biscuit daily.

The pay varies from 2s. 8d. per native serjeant-major to $9\frac{1}{2}d$. for privates. It is slightly increased for every year's service.

Characteristics of Native Soldiers.—The native soldiers are tall and well set up. Their powers of endurance are excellent, and hte men are good marchers, fair shots and are warlike.

The service is popular, and men remain for a long time with the colours.

About two-thirds are Christians and one-third Mohammedans.

Arms, Equipment and Uniform.—Italian officers wear khaki drill jacket, pantaloons and Wolseley pattern helmets. They are mounted on mules about 13 hands high.

The native soldiers wear long white linen coats, and knickers. The headdress is a very high tarbush. Each battalion has a distinctive cummerbund and tassel for the tarbush.

The rifle used in 1911 was the Vetterli Cacano magazine rifle.

Administration.—The military forces of the colony are under the Commandant, who possesses the powers of a divisional general.

He is responsible for the defensive organization of the colony, and for the discipline and training of the troops.

He suggests the distribution of the units to the Governor of the Colony and is generally responsible for all the military administration.

He communicates with the Italian authorities through the Governor of the Colony.

ITALIAN SOMALILAND.

General Description.—The native levies in Italian Somaliland consist at present of 12 infantry companies, 2 machine gun sections, a squadron camel corps, an artillery company and administrative services with headquarters at Mogadisco.

There is also a native police corps with Italian "carabinieri" officers and n.c.os., which has a strength of about 200.

Each infantry company has 5 Italian officers and 446 native soldiers.

The artillery company consists of 1 officer and 90 native soldiers.

The whole force in the country is being gradually raised to 3,500, implying an increase of 15 Italian officers and about 1,000 natives.

Officers.—Officers are seconded from the Italian Army and must serve at least four years. They may be employed in civil duties independently of their military work.

Captains receive £240, lieutenants £192, and artillery lieutenants £216 a year.

After four years' service these sums are increased by one-tenth.

Officers receive extra pay if employed in civilian work.

Rank and File. — The native soldiers are recruited voluntarily amongst the Arabs, the Somalis, and even from the natives of Erithrea and the Yemen.

APPENDIX I.

COMPOSITION OF INFANTRY BRIGADE.

Brigades.	Regiments.	Collar Patch.
Granatieri di Sardegna	1st—2nd Grenadiers	White (collar and cuffs scarlet).
Re	1st—2nd Infantry	Black, edges scarlet.
Piemonte	3rd—4th ,,	Scarlet.
Aosta	5th—6th ,,	Scarlet, central black line.
Cuneo	7th—8th ,,	Crimson.
Regina	9th—10th ,,	White.
Casale	11th—12th ,,	Yellow.
Pinerolo	13th—14th ,,	Black, central scarlet line, scarlet edges.
Savona	15th—16th ,,	White, black central line.
Acqui	17th—18th ,,	Yellow, black central line.
Brescia	19th—20th ,,	Crimson, black central line.
Cremona	21st—22nd ,,	Green, scarlet edges.
Como	23rd—24th ,,	Sky blue.
Bergamo	25th—26th ,,	Sky blue, scarlet central line.
Pavia	27th—28th ,,	Green, scarlet central line.
Pisa	29th—30th ,,	Black, green central line, green edges.
Siena	31st—32nd ,,	Black, yellow edges.
Livorno	33rd—34th ,,	Orange.
Pistoia	35th—36th ,,	Orange, black central line.
Ravenna	37th—38th ,,	White, scarlet edges.
Bologna	39th—40th ,,	White, scarlet central line.
Modena	41st—42nd ,,	White, crimson edges.
Forli	43rd—44th ,,	White, sky blue edges.
Reggio	45th—46th ,,	White, green edges.
Ferrara	47th—48th ,,	Sky blue, scarlet edges.
Parma	49th—50th ,,	Sky blue, white edges.
Alpi	51st—52nd ,,	Green.
Umbria	53rd—54th ,,	Green, white central line.
March	55th—56th ,,	Sky blue, white central line.

APPENDIX I—contd.

COMPOSITION OF INFANTRY BRIGADE—contd.

Brigades.	Regiments.	Collar Patch.
Abruzzi	57th—58th Infantry	Green, black central line.
Calabria	59th—60th ,,	Scarlet, green central line.
Sicilia	61st—62nd ,,	Scarlet, green edges.
Cagliari	63rd—64th ,,	Scarlet, white edges.
Valtellina	65th—66th ,,	Black, white central line, white edges.
Palermo	67th—68th ,,	Black, sky blue central line, sky blue edges.
Ancona	69th—70th ,,	Black, yellow central line, yellow edges.
Puglie	71st—72nd ,,	White, green central line.
Lombardia	73rd—74th ,,	White, sky blue central line.
Napoli	75th—76th ,,	White, crimson central line.
Toscana	77th—78th ,,	Scarlet, white central line.
Roma	79th—80th ,,	Scarlet, yellow edges.
Torino	81st—82nd ,,	Sky blue, yellow central line.
Venezia	83rd—84th ,,	Crimson, sky blue central line.
Verona	85th—86th ,,	Sky blue, yellow edges.
Friuli	87th—88th ,,	Sky blue, black central line.
Salerno	89th—90th ,,	Crimson, white edges.
Basilicata	91st—92nd ,,	Crimson, white central line.
Messina	93rd—94th ,,	Yellow, scarlet edges.

APPENDIX II.

Peace Stations of Alpine Troops (1912).

	Brigade.		Regiment.		Battalion.	
No.	Headquarters.	Number.	Headquarters.	Station.	Name.	
1	Cuneo	1st	Mondovi	Cuneo	Ceva	
				Oneglia	Pieve di Teco	
				Mondovi	Mondovi	
		2nd	Cuneo	Dronero	Borgo San Dalmazzo	
				Cuneo	Dronero	
				Cuneo	Saluzzo	
2	Turin	3rd	Turin	Turin	Pinerolo	
				Pinerolo	Fenestrelle	
				Turin	Exilles	
				Susa	Susa	
		4th	Ivrea	Ivrea	Ivrea	
				Aosta	Aosta	
				Intra	Intra	

		5th	...	Milan	...	Milan	...	Morbegno	...
						Milan	...	Tirano	...
						Milan	...	Edolo...	...
						Bergamo	...	Vestone	...
3	Verona	...	6th	...	Verona	...	Verona	...	Verona	...
						Verona	...	Vicenza	...
						Bassano	...	Bassano	...
		7th	...	Belluno	...	Feltre	...	Feltre...	...
						Padua	...	Pieve di Cadore	...
						Belluno	...	Belluno	...
		8th	...	Udine	...	Tolmezzo	...	Tolmezzo	...
						Udine	...	Gemona	...
						Cividale	...	Cividale	...

APPENDIX III.

Organization into Commands and Districts.

Army Corps Commands.		Divisional Commands.		Military Districts.
No.	Head-quarters.	No.	Head-quarters.	
1	Turin	1	Turin	Turin (41).
				Pinerolo (70).
		2	Novara	Novara (24), Vercelli (75).
				Ivrea (67).
2	Alessandria	3	Alessandria	Alessandria (1), Casale (86).
				Voghera (74), Pavia (54).
		4	Cuneo	Cuneo (40).
				Mondovi (79).
3	Milan	5	Milan	Milan (23), Varese (73).
				Monza (76), Como (22), Lodi (65).
		6	Brescia	Brescia (43).
				Bergamo (42), Lecco (68).
4	Genoa	7	Piacenza	Cremona (44), Piacenza (2), Reggio Emilia (57), Parma (7).
		8	Genoa	Genoa (16).
				Savona (71).
5	Verona	9	Verona	Verona (45), Vicenza (62).
				Mantua (61).
		10	Padua	Padua (29), Treviso (28).
				Belluno (77).
6	Bologna	11	Bologna	Rovigo (63), Venice (51), Sacile (30).
				Bologna (6), Modena (47), Ferrara (55).
		12	Ravenna	Ravenna (8).
				Forli (56).

APPENDIX III—contd.

ORGANIZATION INTO COMMANDS AND DISTRICTS—contd.

Army Corps Commands.		Divisional Commands.		Military Districts.
No.	Head-quarters.	No.	Head-quarters.	
7	Ancona	13	Ancona	Ancona (34), Pesaro (53). Macerata (52).
		14	Chieti	Ascoli Piceno (58), Chieti (9), Foggia (4). Teramo (10), Aquila (48), Sulmona (88), Campobasso (46).
8	Florence	15	Florence	Florence (11). Pistoia (84), Arezzo (49).
		16	Leghorn	Siena (12), Leghorn (13). Lucca (14), Massa (83).
9	Rome	17	Rome	Rome (36). Frosinone (85).
		18	Perugia	Perugia (35), Spoleto (72). Orvieto (69).
		25	Cagliari	Cagliari (15). Sassari (17).
10	Naples	19	Naples	Naples (27), Caserta (26). Benevento (25), Gaeta (64).
		20	Salerno	Salerno (39), Campagna (81). Nola (80), Avellino (50).
11	Bari	21	Bari	Bari (3), Barletta (66), Lecce (5). Taranto (78), Potenza (38).
		22	Catanzaro	Catanzaro (10), Reggio Calabria (21). Castrovillari (82), Cosenza (37).
12	Palermo	23	Palermo	Palermo (33), Cefalu (87). Trapani (32), Girgenti (60).
		24	Messina	Messina (20), Catania (18). Syracuse (59), Caltanis (31).

APPENDIX IV.

SMALL ARM AMMUNITION.

Arm.	On the Man.	Regimental Transport.	Ammunition Columns.	Army Corps Artillery Park.	Total, 1st Line.
Alpine Troops	168	244	90	—	502
Cavalry Division	96	24	74	—	194
Infantry Division	168	24	110	70	372
Bersaglieri	168	24	200	120	512
Corps Cavalry	96	24	60	120	300

2nd Line.

The supply of ammunition in the Army Artillery Park and on the lines of communication is calculated, respectively, at the rate of 30 and 400 rounds per rifle. The actual allotment of these rounds would depend on circumstances, but for purposes of calculation there is no distinction between the different arms of the service.

APPENDIX V.

TABLE SHOWING THE DISTRIBUTION OF RATIONS WITH 1ST LINE ORGANIZATIONS IN THE FIELD.

Organizations.	Rations and Forage.										
	Bread.	Flour.	Groceries.	Meat.	Oats.	Preserved Meat.	Biscuit.	Salt.	Sugar and Coffee.	Pasta risone.	Tobacco.
Mountain Troops — Alpine Troops { On the man	1	—	1	1	2	2	2	2	—	—	3
Alpine Troops { In regimental transport and supply columns	3	—	3	6	6	2	2	2	—	—	3
Total	4	—	4	7	8	4	4	4	—	—	3
Mountain Batteries { On the man	1	—	1	1	2	2	2	2	—	—	3
Mountain Batteries { In battery transport and supply columns	3	—	3	6	6	2	2	2	—	—	3
Total	4	—	4	7	8	4	4	4	—	—	3
Supply column, for groups of Alpine Troops (1)	—	—	3	—	3	—	—	—	—	—	3
Reserve supply park, for groups of Alpine Troops (1)	—	—	—	—	1	2	2	6	6	2	3
Bakery Section, for groups of Alpine Troops (1)	—	4	—	—	—	—	—	4	—	—	—

APPENDIX V—contd.

TABLE SHOWING THE DISTRIBUTION OF RATIONS WITH 1ST LINE ORGANIZATIONS IN THE FIELD—contd.

Organizations.	Rations and Forage.										
	Bread.	Flour.	Groceries.	Meat.	Oats.	Preserved Meat.	Biscuit.	Salt.	Sugar and Coffee.	Pasta risone.	Tobacco.
Cavalry Division											
On the man	1	—	1	1	1	2	2	2	—	—	—
On the saddle	—	—	—	1	1	1	—	—	—	—	—
In the transport of units	1	—	1	—	1	—	—	—	1	—	—
In the cattle park of the supply section	—	—	—	(2)	—	—	—	—	—	—	—
Total	2	—	2	variable	3	3	2	2	—	—	—
Army Corps											
On the man	1	—	1	1	1	2	2	2	—	—	—
In the transport of units	1	—	1	(2)	1	1	—	—	—	—	—
In the cattle park of supply sections	—	—	3	—	—	—	—	—	2	—	—
In the supply column	(3)	(4)	—	—	3	—	—	—	—	—	—
In the bakery section with field ovens (*Weiss* pattern)	1	—	—	—	—	—	—	—	—	—	—
In the army corps supply park	—	—	—	—	(5)2	2	2	2	2	2	—
Total	3	—	5	variable	7	5	4	4	4	2	—

(1) Carries also 1 ration (less meat) per man and 2 rations oats for its own *personnel*.
(2) A number of rations of meat on the hoof according to requirements (drawn from local resources or elsewhere).
(3) If the Army Corps has not got a bakery section with *Weiss* ovens, the supply column carries 3 rations of bread, possibly in biscuit form.
(4) 2 rations of flour are carried for the bakery sections in suitable transport attached to the squads of the advanced supply depôt.
(5) Carries 1 day's oats for the cavalry regiment, the other being carried in nose bags on the saddle.

SCALE OF RATIONS.

Bread, 1 lb. 10½ ozs.
Biscuit-bread, 1 lb. 8·7 ozs.
Flour, 1 lb. ·4 ozs.
Salt for bread, 2·2 drams.
Pasta, *rice* or
Pasta risone } 5·29 ozs.

Salt, 11·2 drams.
Sugar, 11·2 drams.
Coffee, 8·4 drams.
Lard, 8·4 drams.
Pepper, ·28 dram.
Meat, 16⅔ ozs.

Preserved meat, 7·76 ozs.
Biscuit, 14·1 ozs.
Oats, 11 lbs.
Hay, 11 lbs.
Smoking tobacco.
10 cigars for every 3 rations.

Higher Scale of certain Rations for Mountain Troops.

Bread, 2 lbs. 3·27 ozs.
Biscuit-bread, 2 lbs. 1 oz.

Salt, 2·8 drams.
Flour for bread, 1 lb. 10·8 ozs.

Biscuit, 1 lb. 1·6 ozs.

APPENDIX VI.

Peace Stations of Cavalry, 1912.

Divisions.		Brigades.		Regiments.	
Name.	Head-quarters.	Name	Head-quarters.	Names and Numbers.	Head-quarters.
1st Division (Friuli)	Udine	1st	Udine	Saluzzo (12th)	Palmanova
				Monferrato (13th)	Udine
		2nd	Pordenone	Novara (5th)	Treviso
				Milan (7th)	Pordenone
2nd Division (Venetia)	Vicenza	3rd	Vicenza	Genoa (4th)	Padua
				Victor Emanuel II (10th)	Vicenza
		4th	Ferrara	Aosta (6th)	Ferrara
				Mantua (25th)	Bologna
3rd Division (Lombardy)	Milan	5th	Milan	Savoy (3rd)	Milan
				Rome (20th)	Milan
		6th	Parma	Montebello (8th)	Parma
				Vicenza (24th)	Lodi
4*th* Division formed on Mobilization.		7th	Turin	Nice (1st)	Savigliano
				Lucca (16th)	Saluzzo
				Guides (19th)	Voghera
				Catania (22nd)	Turin
				Vercelli (26th)	Vercelli

Note.—A fourth cavalry division is formed on mobilization, and certain of the regiments of the 7th and 8th Brigade as shown will belong to it, but in peace time the regiments shown as forming these brigades are merely inspected and supervised by the Brigade Commanders and do not all form part of the 4th Division. This division will probably be commanded by the Commandant of the Cavalry School at Pinerolo.

APPENDIX VI—contd.

PEACE STATIONS OF CAVALRY, 1912—contd.

Divisions.		Brigades.		Regiments.	
Name.	Head-quarters.	Name.	Head-quarters.	Names and Numbers.	Head-quarters.
		8th	Caserta ...	Foggia (11th) ...	Naples
				Lodi (15th) ...	Aversa
				Piacenza (18th)	Caserta
				Humbert 1st (23rd)	S. Maria Capua Vetere
				Udine (29th) ...	Nola
				Unallotted Regiments—	
				Royal Piedmont (2nd)*	Rome
				Florence (9th)*	Rome
				Alessandria (14th)*	Lucca
				Treviso (28th)*	Florence
				Padua (21st)† ...	Verona
				Caserta (17th)‡	Faenza
				Aquila (27th)§ ...	Brescia

* Inspected and supervized by a Major-General with Headquarters at Rome.
† Inspected by Officer Commanding 3rd Cavalry Brigade.
‡   „   „   „   „   4th   „   „
§   „   „   „   „   5th   „   „

APPENDIX VII.

ORGANIZATION OF THE FORTRESS ARTILLERY.

Regiment.	Regimental Head-quarters.	Groups with Number of Companies in each fortress. c = coast. f = fortress.			
No. I (Coast)	Genoa	c Genoa (3)	c Genoa (3)	c Savona (2)	—
No. II (Coast)	Spezia	c Spezia (3)	c Spezia (3)	c Spezia (3)	—
No. III (Coast and Fortress)	Rome	f Rome (3)	f Rome (2)	f Gaeta (a)	c Maddalena (3)
No. IV (Coast)	Messina	c Messina (4)	c Reggio (3)	c Taranto (3)	c Brindisi (2)
No. V (Coast and Fortress)	Venice	c Venice (3)	c Venice (2) Ancona (1)	f Mestre (2)	—
No. VI (Fortress)	Turin	f Turin (4)	f Turin (3)	f Turin (3)	—
No. VII „	Alessandria	f Alessandria (3)	f Alessandria (3)	f Alessandria (3)	—
No. VIII „	Bologna	f Verona (3)	5 Mantua (3)	f Belluno (3)	—
No. IX „	Verona	f Bologna (4)	f Osoppo (3)	f Conegliano (4)	—
No. X (Siege)	Piacenza	f Piacenza(3)	f Piacenza	f Piacenza(3)	—

194

APPENDIX VIII.

ENGINEERS.

Peace Stations.

Number.	Regiment.	Regimental Headquarters.	Detached Battalions.		
I.	Sappers.	Pavia.	Messina.	—	Rome.
II.	,,	Casale.	Bologna.	—	—
III.	Telegraph.	Florence.	Piacenza.	Mantua.	Verona.
IV.	Pontoons.	Piacenza.	Verona.	—	Venice.
V.	Sappers. Miners.	} Turin.	Treviso.	—	Albenga.
VI.	Railway.	Turin.	Rome.	—	—
"Specialisti" Battalion.	—	Rome.	—	—	—
Aviation Battalion.	—	Turin.	—	—	—

APPENDIX IX.

The Working of the Administrative Services in War.

I. The Intendant-General, who is under the command of the supreme commander, is responsible for the whole of the administrative services.
These include—
>Medical services.
>Commissariat services.
>Telegraph services.
>Postal services.
>Transport and Lines of Communication services.
>Veterinary services.
>Replacement of Artillery including S.A. ammunition and Engineer Stores.
>Carabinieri (Military Police).
>Red Cross representative.

He communicates with the supreme commander, who gives him orders in connection with the intendance; with the War Office as regards the services of supply of stores of all kinds from the interior of the country to the army; and with the army intendants on all administrative questions.

He has a chief of the staff and a staff of officers to carry out his instructions.

II. Every army of two or more army corps has one army intendant, who is responsible under the instructions of the Intendant-General to the army commander for the administrative services of the army.

He has under him:—
>Staff Section.
>Telegraph Direction.
>Post Direction.
>Military Police Direction (Carabinieri).
>Medical Direction.
>Commissariat Direction.
>Transport and Line of Communications Direction.
>Veterinary Direction.
>Artillery Direction.
>Engineer Direction.
>Delegate of the Red Cross Association.

Heads of these various directions may correspond directly on matters affecting them with the similar departments of the Intendant-General.

III. The administrative organizations (stabilimenti) are divided into two subdivisions :—

      Organizations in the field.
         „ reserve.

Organizations in the field are divided into 1st and 2nd Line organizations.

1st Line organizations form part of the divisions, or army corps, and are under the orders of their commanders.

2nd Line organizations are under the orders of the army intendants.

IV. The table facing this page shows the general distribution of the administrative services.

TABLE showing the Distribution

	Directing Authority for all Services.	Distribution.	Medical.	Commissariat.		
				Supply.	Pay.	Clothing and Equipment.
Alpine Troops.	Commanders of the units and their Chief Staff Officers.	1st Line organizations.	Mountain Ambulance. 2 field hospitals (pack transport).	Supply columns. Reserve supply parks, field bakery section, for Alpine group.	—	—
Cavalry Division.			Cavalry Ambulance.	Supply section for cavalry division with cattle park.	—	—
Infantry Division.			Infantry Ambulance.	Supply section with cattle park.	—	—
Army Corps.			Ambulance for corps troops. 6 field hospitals (hospitals from 100–200 beds).	Supply section with cattle park for corps troops. Army corps supply park. Bakery sections with field ovens.	Pay chest of army corps.	Section for supply of boots in connection with army corps clothing park.
Army	Intendence of the Army and Chief of the Staff.	Advanced posts.	Advanced depôt of medical stores, field hospitals of 100 and 200 beds. Hospitals and ambulances of voluntary societies. Hospital trains. Available transport.	Supply section with cattle park. Advanced magazine for supply. Advanced Army Bakeries.	Pay chest of army.	Advanced magazine for supply of clothing and equipment.
		Establishments on L. of C.				
		Intermediate establishments.	Intermediate depôt of medical stores.	Intermediate depôts „ bakery. „ cattle park.	—	—
		Central depôts.	Central depôt of medical stores.	Central depôt „ bakery. „ cattle park.	—	Central depôt for clothing and equipment.
Supreme Command.	General Intendence and Chief of the Staff.		—	—	Pay chest of the Staff of the Intendence-General.	—
In Italy.	War Office.	Reserve Formations.	Territorial medical organizations. Civil medical organizations near the area of concentration. Depôts of the Red Cross.	Territorial supply organizations and centres of manufacture and of business.	Banks under the Treasury.	Military districts near the area of concentration.

(B 10416)

Administrative Services in the Field. [To face p. 107.

Artillery.	Engineers.	Telegraphs.	Post.	Veterinary.	Carabinieri (Mil. Police).	Lines of Communication and Transport.
Ammunition column for Alpine group.	—	—	—	—	—	Baggage column for Alpine group.
Ammunition column.	Bridging section. Mining section.	Telegraph, telephone and wireless sections.	Post office.	—	1 section.	—
Ammunition column.	Company of engineers with park and bridging section.	Telephone park.	Post office.	—	1 section.	—
Ammunition column — artillery park of army corps.	Engineer park of army corps. Searchlight section.	Telegraph company with park.	Post office.	Veterinary stores for replenishing.	Army corps. Headquarters of Carabinieri.	—
Advanced magazine for artillery.	Advanced magazine. Aeronautic section.	Telegraphs.	Postal direction of army.	Veterinary hospitals.	Army headquarters. Carabinieri. 2 sections Carabinieri.	Railway companies with railway sections and park. Automobile park.
						Hqrs. of L. of C. Hqrs. of posts. Entraining office. Hospitals on L. of C. Clothing magazine on L. of C. Bakery on L. of C. Cattle park. Engineer and artillery offices on L. of C. Dep. railway material on L. of C. Remount department on L. of C. Veterinary hospital on L. of C. Carabinieri hospital on L. of C. Military law tribunal on L. of C.
Intermediate artillery and remount depôts.	Intermediate engineer depôt.	—	—	Intermediate veterinary depôt.	—	—
Central depôt for artillery and remounts.	Central engineer depôt.	—	—	—	—	Central depôt for automobile stores.
—	—	Military pigeons.	Hqrs. postal direction and central P.O.	—	Hqrs. Carabinieri — 2 sections.	—
Artillery establishments.	Depôts for stores at regimental headquarters, and material for railways, telegraphs and telephones belonging to the State.		Depôts for postal and telegraphic material under the Minister for Posts and Telegraphs.	Reserve depôt for veterinary stores.	Territorial legions of Carabinieri.	Railway companies. Military railway sections.

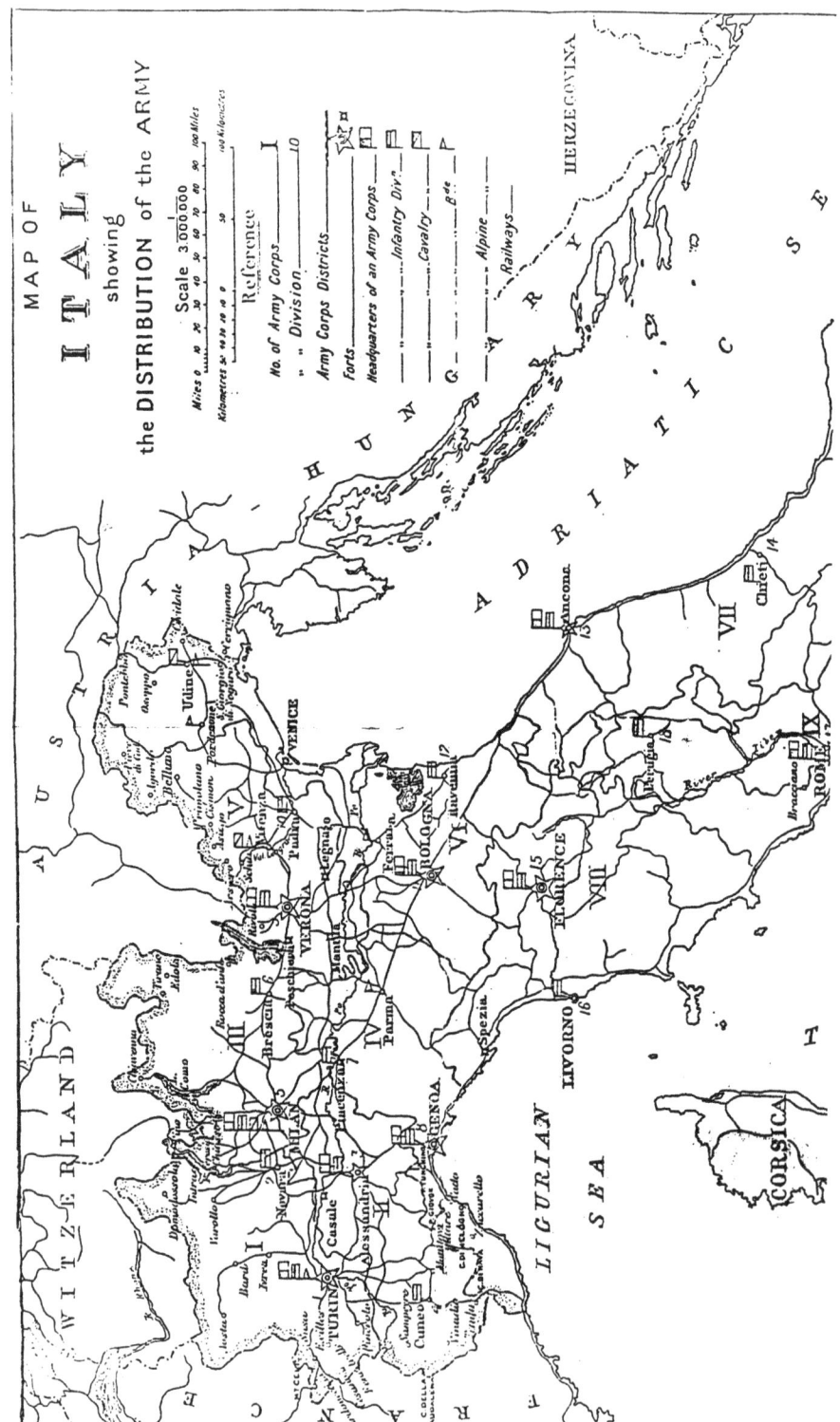

APPENDIX X.

Vocabulary.

I	Io.
Thou	Tu.
He	Egli, Esso—Lui.
We	Noi.
You	Voi.
They	Eglino—Essi.
Who	Chi—Il quale.
What	Che—Che cosa.
Nothing	Nulla—Niente.
Where	Dove.
Hither	Qui— Quá—In Quá.
Here	Qui.
Hence	Da qui.
Thither	Colá.
Never	Mai—Giammai.
My	Mio.
Thy	Tuo.
His	Suo—di lui.
Our	Nostro.
Your	Vostro.
Their	Loro.
Yes	Si.
No	No.
No matter	Non importa.
Whither	Sia che.
Whence	Da dove.
There	Lá.
When	Quando.
To be	Essere.
I am	Sono.
I have been	Sono stato.
To have	Avere.

NUMERALS.

1	... Uno.		17	... Diciasette.
2	... Due.		18	... Diciotto.
3	... Tre.		19	... Diciannove.
4	... Quattro.		20	... Venti.
5	... Cinque.		21	... Vent'uno.
6	... Sei.		30	... Trenta.
7	... Sette.		40	... Quaranta.
8	... Otto.		50	... Cinquanta.
9	... Nove.		60	... Sessanta.
10	... Dieci.		70	... Settanta.
11	... Undici.		80	... Ottanta.
12	... Dodici.		90	... Novanta.
13	... Tredici.		100	... Cento.
14	... Quattordici.		1,000	... Mille.
15	... Quindici.		2,000	... Due mila.
16	... Sedici.		A million	... Un milione.

1st...	... Primo.
2nd...	... Secondo.
3rd...	... Terzo.
4th...	... Quarto.
5th...	... Quinto.
6th...	... Sesto.
7th...	... Settimo.
8th...	... Ottavo.
9th...	... Nono.
10th...	... Decimo.
11th...	... Undecimo.
12th...	... Duodecimo.
13th...	... Decimo terzo.
14th...	... Decimo quarto.
15th...	... Decimo quinto.
16th...	... Decimo sesto.
17th...	... Decimo settimo.
18th...	... Decimo ottavo.
19th...	... Decimo nono.
20th...	... Ventesimo.
21st ...	... Ventesimo primo.
30th...	... Trentesimo.
40th...	... Quarantesimo.
50th...	... Cinquantesimo.
60th...	... Sessantesimo.
70th...	... Settantesimo.
80th...	... Ottantesimo.
90th....	... Novantesimo.
100th...	... Centesimo.
1,000th...	... Millesimo.

Time.

Second	Secondo.
Minute	Minuto.
Hour	Ora.
Half-an-hour	Mezz'ora.
Day	Giorno.
Week	Settimana.
Month	Mese.
Year	Anno.
Morning	Mattina.
Midday	Mezzo Giorno.
Evening	Sera.
Night	Notte.
To-day	Oggi.
Yesterday	Ieri.
To-morrow	Domani.
Sunday	Domenica.
Monday	Lunedi.
Tuesday	Martedi.
Wednesday	Mercoledi.
Thursday	Giovedi.
Friday	Venerdi.
Saturday	Sabbato.
January	Gennaio.
February	Febbraio.
March	Marzo.
April	Aprile.
May	Maggio.
June	Giugno.
July	Luglio.
August	Agosto.
September	Settembre.
October	Ottobre.
November	Novembre.
December	Dicembre.
Spring	Prima vera.
Summer	Estate.
Autumn	Autunno.
Winter	Inverno.

Points of the Compass.

North	Nord, Settentrione.
South	Sud, Mezzo giorno.
East	Oriente, Levante.
West	Ovest, ponente, occidente.

MONEY.

A Franc	Una Lira.
Half a Franc	Mezza Lira.
Five Francs	Cinque Lire.
A Centime	Un Centesimo.
A Halfpenny	Un Soldo.
Money	Denaro.

MILITARY TERMS.

Ranks.

Private	Soldato.
Corporal	Caporale.
Lance-Corporal	Appuntato.
Recruit	Recluta.
Warrant Officer	Maresciallo.
Sergeant	Sergente.
Sergeant (Carabinieri)	Brigadiere.
Sergeant-Major	Furiere Maggiore.
Officer	Ufficiale.
Lieutenant	Tenente.
Captain	Capitano.
Major	Maggiore.
Lieutenant-Colonel	Tenente Colonnello.
Colonel	Colonnello.
General	Generale.

Weapons, &c.

Rifle	Fucile, Moschetto.
Cartridge	Cartuccia.
Bullet	Palla.
Sword	Spada—Sciabola.
Gun	Cannone—Pezzo.
Lance	Lancia.
Powder	Polvere.
Charge (of a gun)	Carica.
Projectile	Proiettile.
Shell	Granata.
Case	Mitraglia.
Shrapnel	Shrapnel.
Trunnions	Orrecchioni.
Breech-piece	Culatta.
Felloe	Quarto.
Spoke	Razzo.
Limber	Avantreno.
Ammunition wagon	Carro per Munizione.
Pole	Timone.
Shafts	Stanghe.

Troops.

Army	Esercito.
Artillery	Artiglieria.
Battalion	Battaglione.
Battery	Batteria.
,, field	,, da Campagna.
,, horse	,, a Cavallo.
,, mountain	,, da Montagna.
,, garrison	,, da Fortezza.
Brigade	Brigata.
Cavalry	Cavalleria.
Company	Compagnia.
Division	Divisione.
Engineers	Genio.
Outposts	Avamposti.
Patrol	Pattuglia.
Regiment	Reggimento.
Rifleman	Bersagliere.
Sapper	Zappatore.
Search-light section	Sezione foto-elettrica.
Sentinel	Sentinella.
Squadron	Squadrone.
Staff	Stato Maggiore.

On the March.

Forward	Avanti.
Street	Strada.
River	Fiume.
Bridge	Ponte.
Hill	Collina.
Railway	Ferrovia.
To the right	A destra.
To the left	A sinistra.
Back	Indietro.
Road	Cammino.
On foot	A piedi.
On horseback	A cavallo.
Wood	Bosco.
Ford	Guado.
Telegraph	Telegrafo.
Signalling	Telegrafia Ottica.
Change of front	Cambiamento di fronte.

In Quarters.

Town	Città.
Church	Chiesa.
Post office	Ufficio Postale.
Mayor	Sindaco.
Magistrate	Magistrato.
Hut	Baracca.
Horse	Cavallo.
Sheep	Pecora.
Fire	Fuoco.
Village	Villaggio.
Inn	Albergo.
House	Casa.
Post master	Maestro di Posta.
Peasant	Contadino.
Interpreter	Interprete.
Shed	Tettoia.
Cow	Vacca.
Pig	Majale.
Candle	Candela.

APPENDIX XI.

Weights and Measures.

The metric measures are used in Italy.

A *useful rule* to convert metres into yards is to multiply the number of metres by 12 and divide by 11,

$$e.g., 100 \text{ metres} = \frac{100 \times 12}{11} \text{ yards.}$$

$$= 109 \text{ yards nearly.}$$

8 kilometres are equal to 5 miles.
10 centimetres are equal to 4 inches.

Measures of Length.

The metric measures of length are :—

(1 millimetre = 0·039370788 inches.)

10 millimetres	=	1 centimetre.
100 ,,	=	1 decimetre.
1,000 ,,	=	1 metre.
10 metres	=	1 decametre.
100 ,,	=	1 hectometre.
1,000 ,,	=	1 kilometre.
10,000 ,,	=	1 myriametre.

British Measures of Length and their Equivalents.

1 inch (pollice)	=	2·54 cm.
1 foot (piede)	=	3·048 dm.
1 yard	=	·9144 m.
1 furlong	=	201·164 m.
1 mile	=	1·6093 km.
12 hands	=	1·22 metres.
14 ,,	=	1·42 ,,
15 ,,	=	1·52 ,,
16 ,,	=	1·63 ,,

Metric Square Measure.

Metric Measures of Superficies.

(1 sq. millimetre (mmq) = 8·00155 sq. inch.)

1 sq. millimetre $= \frac{1}{100}$ sq. centimetre (cmq).

1 sq. centimetre $= \frac{1}{100}$ sq. decimetre (dmq).

1 sq. decimetre $= \frac{1}{100}$ sq. metre (mq).

1 sq. metre $= \frac{1}{100}$ are $= \begin{cases} 10\text{·}7643 \text{ sq. feet.} \\ 1\text{·}196 \text{ sq. yards.} \\ 1550\text{·}06 \text{ sq. inches.} \end{cases}$

1 are = 119·6033 sq. yards.
100 are = 1 hectare (ettaro).
= 2·4711 acres.

British Square Measures and their Equivalents.

1 sq. inch ... ... = 6·4514 cmq.
1 sq. foot ... ... = 9·2899 dmq.
1 sq. yard ... ... = 0·8361 mq.
1 acre ... ... = 0·4047 ettari.
1 sq. mile ... ... = 2·5899 kmq.

Metric Measures of Capacity.

1 millilitre $= \frac{1}{1000}$ litre.

1 centilitre $= \frac{1}{100}$ litre = 0·070439 gill.

1 decilitre $= \frac{1}{10}$ litre.

1 litre = 1·760773 pints = 61·02705 cubic ins.
10 litres = 1 decalitre = 2·2009668 gallons.
100 ,, = 1 hectolitre.
1000 ,, = 1 kilolitre.

British Measures of Capacity and their Equivalents.

4 gills	=	1 pint = 34·66 cubic inches.
2 pints	=	1 quart.
4 quarts	=	1 gallon.
1 gallon	=	4·5435 litres.
1 quart	=	1·1359 ,,
1 pint	=	0·5679 ,,
1 gill	=	0·14198 ,,

Metric Measures of Weight.

1 milligramme	=	0·01544 grains troy.
10 milligrammes	=	1 centigramme.
10 centigrammes	=	1 decigramme.
10 decigrammes	=	1 gramme.
10 grammes	=	1 decagramme.
100 ,,	=	1 hectogramme.
1,000 ,,	=	1 kilogramme.
	=	35·2739 ounces.
100 kilogrammes	=	1 quintal = 1·9684 cwt.
1,000 ,,	=	1 metric ton = ·9842 ton.

British Measures of Weight and their Equivalents.

Avoirdupois Weight.

1 dram	=	1·7718463 grammes.
16 ,,	=	1 oz.
16 oz.	=	1 lb. = 0·4566 kilogrammes.
112 lbs.	=	1 cwt. = 50·8 ,,
20 cwt.	=	1 ton = 1015 ,,

Troy Weight.

1 grain = $\frac{1}{24}$ pennyweight.

1 pennyweight = $\frac{1}{20}$ ounce.

1 ounce = $\frac{1}{12}$ lb.

1 pound = 7000 troy grains.
(15·432349 grains troy = 1 gramme.)

INDEX.

A

	PAGE.
Accounts Office, intendance corps	109
Administration, corps of	114
,, ,, officers	114
,, ,, ,, how recruited	114, 115
,, local	27
,, of army	Chap. II
Administrative services in war	App. IX
Advanced guard	161
Aeronautic services, inspector of	101
Aeroplanes, numbers of	102
,, parks, headquarters of	106
,, squadrons, headquarters of	106
,, ,, organization of	102
,, types of	102
Agriculture, Minister of	125, 127
Air-maps	104
Allowances, officers	136
Alpini, organization of	61–62
,, recruiting for	63
,, troops, peace stations	App. II
Ambulance courses, voluntary	120
Ambulances, field	117, 118
Ammunition, artillery	89, 90
,, cavalry	77
,, for machine guns	108
,, small arms, distribution of	App. IV
Annuities	135

	PAGE.
Area of country	13
Armaments, engineers	98
,, infantry	66, 67
,, of artillery *personnel*	89, 91
,, ,, cavalry	77
,, ,, field artillery	87–89
,, ,, horse artillery	87–89
,, ,, machine gun sections	108
,, ,, medical corps	119
,, ,, mountain artillery	88
,, ,, native troops	180
,, supply companies	115
,, table of, artillery	88, 89
,, transport companies	124
Armies, headquarters of	35
Army bakeries, advanced	113
,, cattle parks	114
,, commander of	35
,, commanders, duties of, in peace	35
,, ,, staff of, in peace	35
,, composition of the forces	17
,, corps commander, duties of	35
,, ,, composition of	34, 42
,, ,, staff of, in peace	35
,, cost of the	135
,, council	26
,, intendants	109
,, ,, offices of	110
,, in the field, composition of	42
,, ,, staff of	42
,, manœuvres, blank ammunition for	142, 144
,, mobilization of	Chap. IV
,, organization of	Chap. IV
,, ,, 1860–64	15
,, ,, 1870–76	16
Artillery brigade	153
,, composition of group of	79, 81, 82
,, construction, inspectorate of	38
,, directions	36, 37
,, directorate of, experiments of	39
,, duties of inspector-general	38
,, field battery	152
,, ,, commands	36
,, formations	152
,, fortress artillery commanders	36

		PAGE.
Artillery, general remarks	... ...	91
,, headquarters of fortress	... ...	36
,, inspector-general of...	... ...	38
,, marching of...	... ...	145
,, native, in Erithrea ...	... ...	177, 178
,, recruits training	... ...	141
,, rounds for annual course ...	... ...	145
,, tactics	... ...	156
,, technical service of ...	... ...	86
,, telephone and signalling classes of	... ...	133
Austrian frontier	... ...	173
,, ,, railways near	... ...	175
Automobile courses	... ...	134
Aviation, aeroplane squadrons	... ...	101, 102
,, battalion	... ...	101, 102
,, courses	... ...	104
,, extra pay for	... ...	104, 105
,, pilots, qualifications for	... ...	104
,, portable sheds for aeroplanes	... ...	106
,, ,, dirigibles	... ...	105
,, schools	... ...	101

B

Baggage, field bakery sections, alpini	... ...	112
,, ,, ,, army corps	... ...	113
,, heavy ...	... ...	167
Balloons, captive	... ...	161
Bari, division at	... ...	44
Battalion, camp for	... ...	169
Battalions, native, in Erithrea	... ...	177
Battery, camp for	... ...	169
Bersaglieri, establishment of ...	... ...	60-61
,, marching of	... ...	142
,, organization of	... ...	60
Billets, general instructions	... ...	168
,, rules for choosing	... ...	168
,, space allowed for	... ...	168
Bivouac, cavalry in	... ...	169
Bridging materials	... ...	98
,, trains ...	... ...	96
Brigade, cavalry, commander of	... ...	35
,, infantry, ,,	... ...	35
,, mountain	... ...	44
Budget ...	... ...	135

(B 10416)

C

	PAGE.
Cadet corps	23
Cadets	128, 129
Cagliari, division at	44
Camps	.169
,, battalion	169
,, battery	169
,, space required by units	170
Canals	175
Carabinieri, armament and equipment	54
,, brigade of...	44
,, description of	50
,, establishment of	51, 52, 53
,, in Erithrea	177
,, N.C.Os. of	55
,, organization of	50
,, pay...	139
,, pensions and reserve pay	140
,, squadrons of	44
,, standard of height for	51
,, terms of service and recruiting for	51
,, war organization of	53
Carbine	77
Categories of service	18
Cavalry against artillery	156
,, ,, infantry	156
,, ambulance	118
,, brigade	151
,, ,, commanders	35, 36
,, charge	155
,, division	43, 151
,, ,, at manœuvres	147
,, ,, details of	43
,, divisional commander, duties of	35
,, formations	149
,, general tactical instructions...	156
,, inspector-general of	37
,, organization of	72
,, peace establishment of	73
,, ,, stations of	App. VI
,, pioneers, course at cavalry school	134
,, preparatory movements in attack	155
,, pursuits	155
,, recent increases in	75
,, reconnaissance	160

	PAGE.
Cavalry regiment, formations of	150
,, ,, peace establishment of	73, 74
,, ,, war establishment	74
,, school	130
,, specially trained N.C.Os. and men in	75
,, squadrons, formations of	150
,, staff of divisions and brigades in peace	72
,, tactics	154
,, tools and explosives carried by	78
,, troop	149, 150
Chargers, officers'	127
Coast artillery courses	132
,, organization of	App. VII
Colonial troops	176–181
,, depôt for	177
,, in Erithrea	177
,, in Libya	176
Commands, organization of	App. III.
Commissariat captains, course at Staff College for	132
,, corps	110
,, directions	37, 110, 111
,, inspector of	39
,, officers, peace establishment	111
,, service in war	112
Communications	171–173
,, telephonic	173
Cooking carts, position on march	167
Courses of instruction—aviation	104
,, ,, miscellaneous	133
Custom guards' duties on frontier	174
,, organization of	23
Cycles, Captain Melli folding	68
,, bersaglieri	68
,, carabinieri	51
Cyclist battalion, organization of	61
,, detachments with cavalry	160
Cyclists, reconnaissance by	159

D

Defence, infantry in	154
,, supreme committee of	26
Defences, land	171
,, maritime	173

		PAGE.
Defences, organization of land	... ...	171
Deport 75 mm. gun		88
Dirigibles, docks for		103
,, types of		103
Disciplinary companies		70, 71
Dismounted action		152
Distance, judging, cavalry		144
,, ,, infantry		143
Districts, organization of		App. III
Division, cavalry, composition of		43
,, command of artillery in		151
,, infantry ,, ...		43
,, militia ,, ...		43
,, Sardinian		44
Divisions, command of		35
Drums not beaten on service		159

E

Education and religion...		14
,, military		Chap. XVI
Emigrants, rules for, liable to military service ...		20
Emigration		13
Engineer commands		37
,, directions		37
Engineers, army corps park, tools of		100
,, ,, park, tools of		100
,, bridging regiment		92, 94, 96
,, ,, train		99
,, divisional bridging section		43, 98
,, field company, tools of		100
,, general description of		92
,, inspector-general of...		38
,, miners' regiment		92, 94, 96
,, miscellaneous badges		98
,, mobile militia companies		97
,, peace stations of		App. VIII
,, railway battalions		96
,, ,, companies, war establishment ...		96
,, ,, regiment		92, 94, 96
,, recruits' training		141
,, sapper regiments		92, 93, 95
,, "specialisti" battalion		93, 94
,, telegraph regiments...		92, 93, 95
,, territorial militia companies		97
,, war establishment of, army corps park ...		95
,, ,, ,, ,, park		95

	PAGE.
Engineers, war establishment of, field company	95
,, ,, ,, pontoon section	95
,, ,, organization of	95
Entrenching tools, field artillery	91
,, ,, mountain artillery	91
,, ,, of infantry	70
Equipment, cavalry	77
,, engineers	98
,, field artillery	90
,, fortress artillery	90
,, horse artillery	90
,, infantry	67
,, mountain artillery	90
,, of native troops	180
,, transport companies	123
,, weight carried at training	142
,, ,, carried in infantry, and alpini	68
Erithrea, administration of	180
,, numbers of colonial troops	178
,, recruiting of colonial troops	178, 179
Expenditure, extraordinary, in Budget	136
,, ordinary, in Budget	135
Expenses, office	138
,, travelling	138
Explosives, carried by cavalry	78
,, ,, engineers	100
,, ,, infantry cyclists	70

F

Farriers' courses	130
Fencing school	133
Field artillery battery war establishment	82
,, ,, courses at School of Gunnery	132
,, ,, increase to	85
,, ,, organization of	80
,, ,, regiment	80, 81, 82
,, firing	143
Firing, instructions for	148
Fortress artillery company	85
,, ,, courses at School of Gunnery	132
,, ,, increase to	86
,, ,, mobile militia	85
,, ,, on mobilization	85

214

	PAGE.
Fortress artillery organization	84
,, ,, ,, of	App. VII
,, ,, territorial militia	85
Fortresses	171, 172
,, naval and military	173
Forts	171, 172
French frontier, railways near	174
Frontier, land	174

G

General Staff, badges of rank for officers	32
,, chief of	28
,, duties of chief of	28, 29
,, establishment of	28
,, general officers on	28
,, intendance division of	30
,, officers of	28
,, operations, division of	29
,, organization of	29
,, pay of	135
,, personnel of	31
,, probationers on	31
,, qualifications of officers for	133
,, secretariat of	29
,, uniform of officers of	31
Geography, Institute of Military	30
Government, form of	13
Grenadier regiment, details of	57, 58
" Guardie di Finanza "	23
Gunnery courses, annual	145
,, School of	132

H

Halts	166
Hangars, portable	105, 106
Heavy artillery battery	84
,, organization	84
Horse artillery, battery	79
,, ,, organization of	79
,, ,, regiment	80
,, breeding establishments	125
,, census	125
,, commissions	126
,, infirmaries, army corps	121
,, ,, garrison	121

		PAGE.
Horses, expenditure on	... ...	127
,, mobilization arrangements	... ...	127
,, peace requirements	... ...	125
,, purchase of	... ...	126
,, quality of	... ...	125
,, Sardinian	... ...	125
,, war requirements	... ...	125
Hospitals, army corps field	... ...	117, 118
,, ,, field ...	... ...	117, 118
,, cavalry division field	... ...	117, 118
,, infantry division field	... ...	117, 118
Hospital ship ...	... ...	120
Howitzer, 149 mm.	... ...	88

I

Infantry ambulance	... ...	118
,, battalion at war strength	... ...	60
,, ,, formations of	... ...	149
,, brigade commanders	... ...	35, 36
,, ,, composition of regiments of	...	App. I
,, ,, formations of	... ...	149
,, company at war strength ...	... ...	60
,, ,, formations of	... ...	148
,, description of	... ...	56
,, divisional commander, duties of ...	... ...	35
,, division, details of ...	... ...	43
,, formations ...	... ...	148, 149
,, light, in Erithrea	... ...	177
,, marching of ...	... ...	142
,, organization of	... ...	56
,, peace establishment of regiment ...	... ...	57, 58
,, periodical change of quarters	... ...	59
,, recruits' training	... ...	141
,, regiment	... ...	149
,, ,, at war strength ...	... ...	60
,, section	... ...	148
,, strength of company, battalion and depôt	...	59
,, tactics	... ...	153
Inspectorate of artillery	... ...	38, 132
Inspectors-General	... ...	37
Intendance corps	... ...	109
,, sub-division of, in peace ...	... ...	109
Intendant-general	... ...	109
,, offices of	... ...	110
Italy, area and population	... ...	13

K

	PAGE.
King's bodyguard	50

L

Lance	77
Lectures	146
Libya, colonial troops in	176

M

Machine gun course at School of Musketry	130
,, ,, section, alpini	107
,, ,, ,, bersaglieri	107
,, ,, ,, cavalry	108
,, ,, ,, infantry	107
,, ,, ,, ,, details of personnel	58
,, ,, ,, position of	149
,, guns	107–108
Magazines, officers in charge of	111
Manœuvres, army	146
,, local	146
,, rules for	147
,, umpires at	147
Map reading	143
Marches, forced, all arms	166, 167
,, length of, all arms	166
,, of mechanical transport	167
,, orders for	168
,, rate of, all arms	165
,, rules for	166
,, time of units passing a given point	170
,, transport on the	167
Marching of recruits	142
Mechanical transport	123, 124
Medical corps, directions of	117
,, ,, establishment of officers	116
,, ,, inspectorate of	117
,, ,, organization in peace	117
,, ,, ,, war	117
,, directions	37
,, officers complementary	116
,, ,, of units	119
,, ,, regular	116

	PAGE.
Medical School, Army...	131
,, services, inspector-general of	39
Melli, Captain, folding bicycle of	68
Messina earthquake	120
Metric system, details of	App. XI
Military Academy	129
,, ,, subjects taught at	129
,, colleges	128
,, districts, duties of staff of	40
,, ,, organization	39
,, ,, personnel for	40
,, engineering, courses for	134
,, forces, development of	14
,, ,, field troops	41
,, ,, garrison troops	41
,, ,, organization for war...	41–44
,, School	128, 129
,, ,, subjects taught at	129
Militia, mobile, composition of	41
,, territorial	41
Minister for War	24
Mobile militia, depôt for	59
Mobilization of army	Chap. IV.
,, rate of, for the various arms	45, 46
,, scheme for	44, 45
,, system of	45
Motor cars, census in Italy of...	124
,, ,, in Libya	123
Mountain ambulance	118
,, artillery battery	82, 83
,, ,, ,, war establishment	83
,, ,, increase to...	85
,, ,, on mobilization	83
,, ,, organization of	82
,, brigade, composition of	44
,, troops, details of	43
,, ,, inspector-general of	38
Mules, supply of...	127
Musketry, cavalry	144
,, infantry	142–143
,, recruits	143
,, rounds allowed annually	142, 143
,, School of	130
,, targets used at	143
,, winter training in	143

N

	PAGE.
Native soldiers in Erithrea, characteristics of	180
Naval harbours, first class	173
Navy, personnel for coast defences	173
Non-commissioned officers, ranks of	49
,, privileges of	49
,, promotion of	49
,, retirement of	49
Nurses	120

O

Officers, allowances of	137, 138
,, badges of rank	65
,, categories of	47
,, medical, complementary	116
,, ,, of units	118
,, ,, regular	116
,, on half-pay, &c.	47
,, pay of	136, 137
,, promotion of	47
,, ranks of	47
,, reserve of	48
,, staff, promotion of	31
,, where obtained	47
Organization of army	Chap. IV
,, commands and districts	Chap. III
Outposts	162
,, cyclists for	162
,, flags of truce	165
,, general control of area	164
,, march	165
,, observation posts	164
,, orders for	164
,, outpost reserves	163, 164
,, piquets	163
,, sentries	163
,, supports	163

P

Patrols, duty of	160
Pay, carabinieri	139
,, colonial troops in Erithrea	179

Pay, extra, for aviation	104-5
„ „ of officers at Rome	137
„ native troops in Erithrea	180
„ N.C.Os. and rank and file	139, 140
„ of officers in Somaliland, Italian	181
„ officers	136
Pensions...	135, 136, 138, 140
„ and reserve pay, under officers	140
„ war	138
Pigeon post	75
Pinerolo...	130
Pontoon brigades	96
Population	13
Promotion, central committee of	26
„ test course for captains	134
Protection, duty of	161
„ on the march	161

Q

Quadrilateral Italian fortress...	172

R

Railway committee, military	30
„ courses	134
Railways	174
„ light	175
Rations	App. V
„ and forage, 1st line organizations	App. V
„ carried by advanced supply depôts	113
„ „ army cattle parks	114
„ „ reserve army supply parks	114
„ for mountain troops	191
„ in the field	App. V
„ scale of...	App. V
Rear guard	162
Reconnaissance	159
„ dirigibles, captive balloons and aeroplanes for	161
„ use of engineers	161
Reconnaissances, local...	160
Recruiting, colonial troops	178, 180
„ peculiarities of system	21-22
Recruits, categories of the annual classes of...	18, 19
„ distribution of	21

220

	PAGE.
Red Cross Society	119, 120
„ organizations of	120
Re-engaged men	20
Rejections of men from military service	20, 21
Remount depôts	125, 126
„ squadrons	126
Reserve army supply parks	114
Roads	175
Rolling stock	175

S

Sardinian army	14
School for sub-lieutenants of artillery and engineers ...	131
Service, conditions of	17
„ dress, see Uniform.	
„ terms of	18
Small arms committee	130
Somaliland, Italian, native levies in	180
„ „ recruiting of native levies	181
„ „ strength of troops in	181
Spingardi general, army reforms introduced by	16
Squadron, native, in Erithrea	178
Staff College	132
„ „ course at	132
„ „ „ for commissariat officers	111
„ „ entrance examination	132
„ tour of chief of the general staff	146
„ tours	146
Stallions, importation of	125
Starting points	168
Strength of army, peace and war	22
Supply columns, alpini	112
„ „ army corps	113
„ companies	110, 112
„ depôts, advanced	113
„ park, army corps	113
„ parks, alpini, reserve	112
„ „ reserve army	114
„ sections	112
„ service, 1st line organizations	112, 113
„ „ 2nd „ „	113, 114
Swiss frontier, railways near	174
Sword, cavalry	77

T

	PAGE.
Tactics	Chap. XIX
,, general tendencies of	157, 158
Telegraph parks	95
Telephone and signalling course	133
,, ,, courses	134
Telephotography	104
Territorial legions of carabinieri	50
Tools carried by cavalry	78
Tor di Quinto, cross-country riding course at	130
Training, annual course of	141
,, field	146
,, of artillery	145
,, ,, cavalry	143
,, ,, infantry	141
,, recruits course of	141
Transport, 1st line	167
,, alpini	69
,, cavalry on the march	157
,, columns, auxiliary	123
,, companies, distribution of	122
,, ,, of engineers	96
,, company, expansion for war	123
,, ,, peace establishment of	122
,, field artillery battery	91
,, for cavalry regiment	78
,, ,, fighting	167
,, heavy baggage	167
,, infantry and bersaglieri	68, 69
,, mechanical	123, 124
,, mountain artillery battery	91
,, of aeroplane squadrons	102
,, ,, engineers bridging train	100
,, ,, ,, field company	99
,, ,, ,, telegraph park	99
,, ,, troops by rail, central commission of	30
,, office intendance corps	109
,, organization	122, 123
,, position on march	167
,, system, efficiency of	123
Trumpet calls not used on service	159

U

	PAGE.
Under officers at the Military School	129
,, definition of	49
Uniform, Alpini	65
,, and equipment, transport companies	123
,, artillery	87
,, badges of rank	65
,, ,, worn by aviation officers	104
,, bersaglieri	64, 65
,, carabinieri	54
,, cavalry	76
,, commissariat corps	115
,, corps of administration	115
,, engineers	97
,, general staff	31, 32
,, grenadiers and infantry	63
,, medical corps	119
,, miscellaneous badges in	66
,, native troops	180
,, service dress for grenadiers and infantry	64

V

Venice, lagoon companies at	96
Veterinary corps, establishment of	120
,, officers with units	121
,, training course	130
Vocabulary, Italian	App. X
Volunteer corps	23
Volunteers	19

W

War games	146
,, Office	24–25
Weiss ovens	113

www.ingramcontent.com/pod-product-compliance
Ingram Content Group UK Ltd.
Pitfield, Milton Keynes, MK11 3LW, UK
UKHW041303180426
11947UKWH00009B/660